audition speeches
for young actors 16+

JEAN MARLOW   SECOND EDITION

Methuen Drama

To Bill Germano 'Thank you'

First published 2006

Methuen Drama
A & C Black Publishers Limited
38 Soho Square
London W1D 3HB
www.acblack.com

© 2006 Jean Marlow

ISBN-10: 0-7136-7889-5
ISBN-13: 978-0-7136-7889-5

A CIP catalogue record for this book is available from
the British Library.

This book is produced using paper that is made from wood
grown in managed, sustainable forests. It is natural, renewable
and recyclable. The logging and manufacturing processes conform
to the environmental regulations of the country of origin.

Typeset in 9.75 on 12pt Garamond and 9 on 11 pt DIN

Printed and bound in Great Britain

JEAN MARLOW

Jean Marlow LGSM, a qualified speech and drama teacher (Guildhall School of Music and Drama), is also an actress and writer with many years' experience in theatre, films and television.

She began her career at the Palace Theatre Watford as a student Assistant Stage Manager, playing small parts. There she played 'Button' in *Housemaster* and went on to work at the Theatre Royal, Northampton, where she was the young schoolgirl 'Julia' in *Daddy Longlegs*. Even after graduating to 'grown-up' roles she went on to work for The Unicorn Children's Theatre at the Arts Theatre, London, playing the Leading Hen – 'Mrs Short-And-Long' – in *A Fox and His Drum*. It was the first time she had had to sing and dance on stage and remembers doing 'a lot of jumping about and squawking'.

In more recent years she played 'Mrs Ebury' in Tom Stoppard's *Dirty Linen* in the West End, and Doll Common in *Playhouse Creatures*. She also played a leading part, 'Mrs Turner', in the award-winning film *The Little Ones*, and 'Mrs Jiniwin' in the Walt Disney series *The Old Curiosity Shop* with Peter Ustinov and Tom Courtenay. She was 'Miss Prism' in the Number One tour of *The Importance of Being Earnest*, and 'Winnie Winger' the stunt pilot in an episode of *Jay Jay The Jet Plane*, a new series for childrens' television.

Her other books include: *Audition Speeches for All Ages and Accents*, *Classical Audition Speeches*, *Duologues for All Accents and Ages*, *Audition Speeches for Men/Women* and *Audition Speeches for 6–16 Year Olds*.

She is Co-Director of the Actors' Theatre School, and it is her untiring search for suitable audition speeches for our students of varying ages and nationalities that brought about these books.

EAMONN JONES
FOUNDER DIRECTOR
THE ACTORS' THEATRE SCHOOL

contents

acknowledgements xi
preface 1
introduction 3

why go to drama school 5
Tim Reynolds, Principal of the Academy Drama School 5
Roland Rees, Theatre Director and founder of the
Foco Novo Theatre Company 7
Robert Croucher, President of the American Academy of
Dramatic Arts, New York 8

developing extra skills 9
Tona de Brett, ARCM, Singing coach 9
Sylvia Carson, Actress and choreographer 10

more about auditioning 12
Anji Carroll, Casting director for theatre, film and television 12
Gabrielle Dawes, Deputy Casting Director, National Theatre 13

out on your own 15
Alan Ayckbourn, Playwright and Artistic Director of the
Stephen Joseph Theatre, Scarborough 15
Vicky Ireland, Artistic Director, Polka Theatre for Children 16
Jonathon Siddall, Artistic Director, Hampstead Theatre 18

advice from the actors 19
Pat Keen 19
Michael Conrad 20
Rebecca Callard 20

a word about the speeches 22
Choosing a speech 22
Shakespeare's Plays 23
   Valerie King BA (Hons) Cert Ed, LLAM (Hons), LGSM
   Head of Drama, Laine Theatre Arts; Examiner for the London
   Academy of Music and Dramatic Art (LAMDA) .24

audition speeches for men 25

audition speeches for women 71

more ideas for speeches:
    men 129
    women 135

useful addresses 141

copyright holders 143

audition speeches for men

Wint Selby   **AH! WILDERNESS** EUGENE O'NEILL 26

Guy Bennett   **ANOTHER COUNTRY** JULIAN MITCHELL 28

Serpent   **BACK TO METHUSELAH**
GEORGE BERNARD SHAW 30

Freddie   **A BRIEF HISTORY OF HELEN OF TROY OR
EVERYTHING WILL BE DIFFERENT**
MARK SCHULTZ 32

Morgan Evans   **THE CORN IS GREEN** EMLYN WILLIAMS 34

Honey   **CRESSIDA** NICHOLAS WRIGHT 36

Billy   **THE CRIPPLE OF INISHMAAN**
MARTIN MCDONAGH 38

Sloane   **ENTERTAINING MR SLOANE** JOE ORTON 40

Steve   **FLATMATES** ELLEN DRYDEN 42

Tom   **THE GLASS MENAGERIE**
TENNESSEE WILLIAMS 44

Youngblood   **JITNEY** AUGUST WILSON 46

Raleigh   **JOURNEY'S END** R C SHERRIFF 48

Harry   **LOVE ON THE DOLE**
RONALD GOW AND WALTER GREENWOOD 50

Puck   **A MIDSUMMER NIGHT'S DREAM**
WILLIAM SHAKESPEARE 52

Moses   **MONSIEUR IBRAHIM AND THE FLOWERS
OF THE QUR'AN** ERIC-EMMANUEL SCHMITT . . .54

The Templar   **NATHAN THE WISE**
GOTTHOLD EPHRAIM LESSING 56

Mark   **NEW BOY** WILLIAM SUTCLIFFE 58

Romeo   **ROMEO AND JULIET**
WILLIAM SHAKESPEARE 60

Lee	**SCHOOL PLAY** SUZY ALMOND 62	
Tony Lumpkin	**SHE STOOPS TO CONQUER** OLIVER GOLDSMITH 64	
Oggy Moxon	**TEECHERS** JOHN GODBER 66	
Dog	**THE WITCH OF EDMONTON** THOMAS DEKKER, JOHN FORD & WILLIAM ROWLEY 68	

audition speeches
for women

Agnes	**AGNES OF GOD** JOHN PIELMEIER	72
Lulu	**ALL THE ORDINARY ANGELS** NICK LEATHER	74
Joni	**ANCIENT LIGHTS** SHELAGH STEPHENSON	76
Charlotte	**A BRIEF HISTORY OF HELEN OF TROY OR** **EVERYTHING WILL BE DIFFERENT** MARK SCHULTZ	78
Grusha	**THE CAUCASIAN CHALK CIRCLE** BERTOLT BRECHT	80
Nicola	**CITY SUGAR** STEPHEN POLIAKOFF	82
Margaret Knox	**FANNY'S FIRST PLAY** GEORGE BERNARD SHAW	84
Lynn	**FLATMATES** ELLEN DRYDEN	86
Mabel Chiltern	**AN IDEAL HUSBAND** OSCAR WILDE	88
Rena	**JITNEY** ANGUS WILSON	90
Angela	**LIKE A VIRGIN** GORDON STEEL	92
Girleen	**THE LONESOME WEST** MARTIN MCDONAGH	...94
Sally	**LOVE ON THE DOLE** RONALD GOW AND WALTER GREENWOOD	96
Frankie	**MEMBER OF THE WEDDING** CARSON MCCULLERS	98
Mercy	**MERCY FINE** SHELLEY SILAS	100
Frehia	**MERCY FINE** SHELLEY SILAS	102
Rachel	**NATHAN THE WISE** GOTTHOLD EPHRAIM LESSING	104
Carol	**OLEANNA** DAVID MAMET	106
Mary Mooney	**ONCE A CATHOLIC** MARY O'MALLEY	108
Sally Stokes	**THE PASSING-OUT PARADE** ANNE VALERY	...110

Eliza Doolittle   **PYGMALION** GEORGE BERNARD SHAW 112

Lucy   **THE RIVALS** RICHARD BRINSLEY SHERIDAN . .114

Juliet   **ROMEO AND JULIET**
WILLIAM SHAKESPEARE 116

Charlie   **SCHOOL PLAY** SUZY ALMOND 118

Heavenly   **SWEET BIRD OF YOUTH**
TENNESSEE WILLIAMS 120

Ruby   **WHEN WE ARE MARRIED** J B PRIESTLEY 122

Lue   **THE WINTERLING** JEZ BUTTERWORTH 124

Tina   **THE WOMAN BEFORE**
RICHARD SCHIMMELFENNIG 126

more ideas for speeches: men

Mozart   **AMADEUS** PETER SCHAFFER 130

Carl   **MADAME MELVILLE** RICHARD NELSON 131

Derek   **ONCE A CATHOLIC** MARY O'MALLEY 132

George   **PRESENCE** DAVID HARROWER 133

Andi   **THE WOMAN BEFORE**
ROLAND SCHIMMELPFENNIG 134

more ideas for speeches: women

Linda   **ENTER A FREE MAN** TOM STOPPARD 136

Pearl   **HOUSE AND GARDEN** ALAN AYCKBOURN 137

Elke   **PRESENCE** DAVID HARROWER 138

Maire   **TRANSLATIONS** BRIAN FRIEL 139

Pace   **THE TRESTLE AT POPE LICK PARK**
NAOMI WALLACE 140

acknowledgements

I would like to say thank you to the actors, directors, playwrights, casting directors, teachers, agents and organisations who have helped me with this book, and especially:

Brian Schwartz and the Offstage Bookshop, Roger Croucher of the American Academy of Dramatic Arts, Betty Lawson, Alan Ayckbourn, Tim Reynolds, Roland Rees, The Royal Academy of Dramatic Art, Gabrielle Dawes, Anji Carroll, Patrick Young, Vicky Ireland, Sylvia Carson, Tona de Brett, Valerie King, actors Pat Kean, Rebecca Callard and Michael Conrad, Julia McDermott, Rona Laurie, Serena Hill, The Royal National Theatre, Ed Berman of Inter-Action, Jacky Matthews, Tom Stoppard, James Hogan of Oberon Books, Amanda Smith, Samuel French Ltd, Kevin Daly, Jacky Leggo, Matt Plant, Mary Holland, Frances Cuka, Carol Schroder, Heather Stoney, Ellen Dryden, Sheila Killeen, Keith Salberg, Margaret Hamilton and the students of the Actors' Theatre School, my Co-director Eamonn Jones, my publishers A & C Black – and not forgetting my editors, Jenny Ridout and Katie Taylor.

preface

The Frankfurt Book Fair has always intrigued me. It happens once a year and, although my Editor assures me it is not all that exciting, it was here that the idea for this new book came about. 'There is a definite need for a book of audition speeches for the 16+ age-group,' they said. 'These younger actors are being left out.' So I began to investigate – and they were right. There are lots of good audition books for older actors and a few for children from eight to 16 – but the group in the middle is being squeezed out. And yet young actors applying for full-time drama school are urged to present audition speeches suitable for their own age and capabilities, and external drama examinations for the London New Era Academy of Music and Dramatic Art (LAMDA) and the Guildhall School of Music and Drama look for the same thing. Most of the extracts in this book are drawn from characters under the age of 20 and some, like 'Frankie' in *Member of the Wedding*, are under 16 but require an actor a couple of years older to perform them.

Looking through casting requirements recently, particularly for younger actors, it's amazing to see how multi-talented you need to be these days. Many performers in Small Scale and Number One touring productions are expected to be able to sing, dance, play an instrument and even have circus skills. The younger members of the cast of The Good Company's *Hard Times* threw themselves into back somersaults, and one of them swung upside down on a trapeze! So I asked actress and choreographer Sylvia Carson, and singing coach Tona de Brett, to talk about developing special skills. Auditioning itself could almost be counted as a 'special skill' and I have also included some excellent advice from casting directors Gabrielle Dawes (Royal National Theatre) and Anji Carroll (television's *London's Burning* and currently *The Wizard of Oz*, Bristol Old Vic Theatre).

All these speeches have been tried and tested by students from the Actors' Theatre School and presented not only in their End of Term shows, but also at outside auditions and LAMDA New Era examinations – so we know they work!

I hope these books will be helpful both to students and to young professional actors alike, and perhaps be a reminder of the many good plays seen in London and the provinces today – and often too briefly on the fringe.

1

introduction

'It's different at different times . . . When you're young, you're just
a child being clever. Then it changes . . . Then you get older. When
other boys get tall and clumsy. And their voices drop two million
pegs. We don't do that. We hang on . . . It's like a baby falling
down a well. You've got its foot in your hand and you don't let go.
So you're not one thing exactly. You're half man, half boy. That's
when you find out you can really do it. And it's amazing . . . You
come on stage and everything happens the way it's meant to . . . '

Honey in *Cressida* by Nicholas Wright

Many younger actors reading this book will have attended stage school
– some from the ages of eight to 16 – and already worked in theatre,
films or television. Others will have done drama at school, maybe for
GCSEs or A Levels and taken part in End of Term plays. So they'll understand exactly how 'Honey', a boy actor who had grown up with The
King's Men theatre company, feels. Parents and friends praise you; you
enjoy performing and you want to carry on. You don't want to 'let go'!

Of course, everyone knows of someone who, like 'Honey', was in the
right place at the right time and was handed out all the starring roles.
And luck can play a large part in determining your future career.

I'd only just started working and was given a tiny part in an episode
of a new television series. During rehearsals I got talking to a young
actress, 'Frances', who was playing a leading part and she started to tell
me about her 'Lucky Break'. She was on her way to audition for a part
in a West End play, when she stopped to help an old lady who had
something in her eye. She knew it would make her late for her appointment but she couldn't just leave the poor woman standing there. So she
got whatever it was out of her eye and then found her a taxi. When she
arrived at the audition she was made to wait, as several other actors had
gone in ahead of her. It was so late it was unlikely she would even be
seen. But she was finally called and as she walked on stage there, to her
amazement, she saw the 'old lady' she had helped sitting in the auditorium. It was Yvonne Arnaud, the famous French actress and star of the
production. Frances auditioned and was given the part. After this, of
course, she was in great demand not only for theatre work, but also for
films and television.

I've thought a lot about her since I was asked to do this book. Would
I have got the part if it had been me at that particular time? The answer

is 'No'. I wasn't ready. Frances was an extremely good actress and well qualified to play the part. She'd studied hard at drama school and had already played smaller parts in good repertory theatres. She'd worked on her voice and – most important of all – she could be heard easily at the back of a large auditorium.

So it's no good just sitting at home day-dreaming. If you are basing your career simply on luck then you're likely to be disappointed. On the other hand, if you work hard, keep your voice in good shape and try to develop as many extra skills as possible, when the opportunity comes along you will be ready to take it. You'll arrive at your audition, walk on stage and 'everything will happen the way it's meant to'.

why go to drama school?

In the early 17th century, young boys were kidnapped by unscrupulous managements, put into lodgings and, if no one turned up to claim them, *forced* to work in the theatre. There they were taught to speak lines, exercise their voices and, after each performance, study new scripts overnight ready for the next production. Today you'd have to pay substantial fees to get anything like that amount of experience. And yet a good all-round training is essential if you are to survive for long in an extremely competitive and overcrowded business.

Drama schools in Great Britain tend to be expensive, so it is as well to look carefully through the various prospectuses, not only to see what will be required of you at the audition, but also to make sure you can afford the school of your choice. Not all local councils – or in the case of students overseas, governments – are prepared to assist you these days. However, some schools are now offering degree courses (BA Drama) and most councils are inclined to look more favourably on these. A few universities also offer BA Drama degrees, but these are mainly academic.

In the United States there are very few vocational drama schools like the Royal Academy of Dramatic Art (RADA) or the Guildhall School of Music and Drama in London. Perhaps the equivalent would be the Juilliard School or the American Academy of Dramatic Arts in New York. Most drama courses are affiliated to universities, such as Yale, and are again very expensive. There are no grants available although you may qualify for a student loan. If you decide to go to drama school there are scholarships you can apply for, or you could approach one of the various Foundations for a theatre bursary.

TIM REYNOLDS, Principal of the Academy Drama School, White-chapel, has this advice for would-be drama students:

'Why did you buy this book? There may have been lots of reasons. You could be in a class already, or with a private tutor, and be preparing to do an exam such as LAMDA or Guildhall; or you could finally have made your mind up to enter, for better or worse, our acting profession.

If you know that this is what you want more than *anything* else in the world, and that *nothing* in the world can stop you, then you must be prepared to give everything to it – just as the dedicated future sportsperson knows that they have to train continually. If you want to exercise more control over the ball, or if you want to be the best in your swimming team, you have to keep toning up the muscles and preparing yourself to be the best. As a student dancer or singer must practise for hours at a time, so must you. You have chosen the acting profession. The rules are no different.

So how do you use this excellent book of speeches from plays? Well, let's assume that you have an audition coming up. Perhaps for an amateur production, or maybe for drama school. Where do you turn for speeches? If you're auditioning for drama school, you will be expected to learn two at least. Over the years our experience has taught us that most drama schools require one modern and one Shakespeare (or classical), but some will require a "set" speech to be learned as well. Most of us have got a Complete Works about somewhere, and have either seen or read at least a few of Shakespeare's plays. There are some excellent classical speeches in this book, but what about the modern piece? Here you will find an excellent and well-chosen selection to suit any student actor.

Remember that these speeches are only a section of the play. What has your character done or lived through before the speech begins? What will he or she go on to do afterwards? Once you find the speech that you feel is most right for you, you must buy and carefully read a copy of the play, classical or modern. Look very carefully at the requirements for the audition, and make sure you follow them to the letter. When you get there you must listen to the instructions given, and follow them. The most important piece of advice I can give is: know your speeches thoroughly, and above all, *be on time*.

Drama schools are notoriously hard to get into, as the supply greatly exceeds the demand. They are looking for the right people for their course, so you may be talented but not the right kind of student for their style of training. Rejection is part of an actor's life; try not to be crushed by it and just keep going.

Here at the Academy in Whitechapel we run a foundation course called the Medallion Course – a one-year preparation dedicated to getting would-be actors into drama school. Although not a full training in itself, it prepares students thoroughly for training at drama school while teaching the principles of voice, movement, film and TV work, armed and unarmed combat, etc. They have a chance to perform at the end of each term, and prepare, through a series of tests and mock auditions. They also meet graduate students who can tell them more about the drama school of their choice. This may be the way to go for you, but whether it is or not, I wish you every success in your chosen profession.'

The Royal Academy of Dramatic Art (RADA) auditions between 1400 and 1500 students a year for 30 available places. Auditions are held in London and New York. The Principal, Nicholas Barter, looks particularly for commitment and trainability when auditioning younger (18-year-old) students, 'not just those with nice middle-class voices and a few acting medals taken at school'.

ROLAND REES has worked extensively throughout the theatre in the UK. He has directed plays for leading repertory theatres, commercial theatre and the Royal National Theatre, and was the founder and Artistic Director of the Foco Novo Theatre Company. He also directed a new play, *Kit's Play*, commissioned from Howard Brenton for the Royal Academy of Dramatic Art:

'At the end of the day, self-confidence and of course talent are irreplaceable. If an actor had something inside which a director clocks, there is an immediate connection. Different directors click with different actors.

Repertory companies used to be the training ground for young actors. They joined a company for a good period of time and immersed themselves in a hierarchy of age and experience. They may have been to drama school but here, within a company of peers of their profession, they learnt at first hand their trade. In this situation an actor's look had to suit many parts.

Now, no such companies exist within the repertory system. A theatre programme runs project by project, the content of which is as much determined by the definitions of grant and sponsorship applications as it is by the artistic drive behind the programme. In this situation an actor's look is chosen for one specific part.

Nick Barter at RADA explained to me that he changed his three-year course so that actors in their final year almost exclusively acted in plays. Two in each term. The period of training was phased out in exchange for the experience of preparing a part. This was directly in response to the loss of the repertory company.

The commerciality of the business has become paramount, even in the parts which receive subsidy and public sponsorship. Theatre itself has become reconstructed in the form of film and TV. Nick Barter finds at RADA that predatory agents are culling his boys and girls onto their books at the start of Year Three. Many get offered film and TV parts. One, this year, made a film in their second year, presently on release. It is hard for Nick Barter to resist these opportunities for his students, but in some cases he justifiably puts his foot down.

So the audition has become more and more to do with casting for one-off events, particularly for those entering the profession. An actor is looked at as a specific for the auditioned part, the director's view of that part and their interior view of the look of the project.

7

Which brings us back to talent and confidence, because an actor cannot alter these givens. No more is an actor chosen for their 'company' commitment – indeed they may be notoriously difficult – but for their specificity. And only for a brief duration.

Add to the gloss of the audition this – an actor's bankability, which in many cases involves younger and younger actors, soon after they leave drama school. And remember that a so-called "ugly" actor can be bankable.

Going into an audition
Think
I am good, am good, am good.
But don't swamp the director. Be yourself.
Create your own space.
The director is there to "colonise" the meeting.
Leave a memory.'

ROGER CROUCHER – President of the American Academy of Dramatic Arts in New York, has this to say:

'The general admission policy of the American Academy of Dramatic Arts is to admit all artistically and academically qualified individuals who appear to be mature and sufficiently motivated for conservatory training. During the audition/interview, special attention is given to the applicant's emotional connection to the material and his or her ability to listen in the real-world context of the interview, since good listening is fundamental to good acting. Other criteria include sensitivity, a sense of humour, feel for language, vocal quality, vitality, presence, cultural interests and a realistic understanding of self and the challenges involved in pursuing an acting career.

At the Academy, classical audition material is seen as presenting an untrained actor with an exceptional challenge: to speak lines far removed from everyday conversation – but frequently rich with wit, poetic imagery and exalted emotion – with the same quality of honest, personal connection that is desirable when speaking lines from simple, more contemporary material.

Even though untrained actors may not have the vocal development and verbal skills to do full justice to classical material, they can use it effectively in auditions. They should speak the lines clearly and simply, without false emotions or undue emphasis on perfect speech and vowel sounds, while keeping in mind that the character is a human being with something to say and a reason for saying it.'

developing extra skills

Nowadays it's not enough to go to drama school and hope that when you leave there will be a job waiting for you. Try and develop extra skills, both before and after drama school, that will make you more 'castable'.

Agent **Jacky Leggo** says 'it is much easier to find work for young people who can sing'. And a look at recent casting requirements on the Equity Job Information list confirms this. Many drama schools will ask you to prepare a song for your audition, particularly if you are recalled, and most ask for movement and improvisation at the beginning of the session. It's no good standing up and singing 'Three Blind Mice', as one of my students did. Nobody expects you to be an expert singer but they like to think that you've made an effort to present your song properly. And it is well worthwhile taking a few singing lessons.

TONA DE BRETT, ARCM, has taught voice productions for many years to a wide range of artists, including classical singers, actors and pop/rock singers. She has taken classes in Musical Comedy at the City Lit and in other adult education centres. Her pupils have included Johnny Rotten, Ozzie Osborne, Paul Young, Val Kilmer, Rick Moranis, Jimmy Nail, Courtney Love, John Taylor, Skin, Basia, Martine McCutcheon, Dido and many more. Her book *Discover Your Voice* includes a CD of vocal exercises and is published by Schott & Co.:

'Singing has always been an essential part of the actors' stock in trade. From the court jester to the most avant garde musicals – through elegant operettas and bawdy music hall – actors are expected to handle them all. However, it is not enough to be the possessor of a good voice. You must be able to use your voice skilfully and confidently and therefore it is necessary to learn the technique of voice production. You will then be able to sing many roles and to cope with different situations, even singing through coughs and colds. Of course, if you are ill, ideally rest is best; but there are times when "the show must go on".

Keeping fit is vital. Take regular physical exercise, eat sensibly and regularly, don't smoke or indulge in recreational drugs or heavy drinking. Your body is your instrument after all, and the better you treat it the better your voice will be.

Find a teacher whom you like and whose opinion you trust. You will often hear of a good teacher through friends or through a singer you admire. Your teacher will help you with breath control and tone production and will encourage you to discover the amazing resonances that your voice creates in the body. Good singing feels wonderful to the performer and the listener alike.

Warm up with a series of vocal exercises before you practise your songs or give a performance. Your teacher should recommend suitable exercises or you can use various recorded exercises. I have a collection of my own that many people use and enjoy.

Care for your voice with respect and affection and it will never let you down.'

Sylvia Carson – actress and choreographer, has worked in theatres in the West End, all over the British Isles and also in Canada, most recently playing 'Muriel Wickstead' in *Habeus Corpus*, 'Lady Caroline' in *A Woman of No Importance*, 'Fairy Godmother' in *Cinderella* and 'The Housekeeper' in *The Late Edwina Black*. She has choreographed or been Movement Director for many musicals and plays including *Dancing at Lughnasa* and the English premiere of *Bondagers* as well as producing corporate events. She teaches movement and takes choreographic workshops in England, Italy and the USA:

'Some basic movement training has always been included in drama training but sometimes taken under sufferance by the would-be actors as irrelevant. However, today it is essential. Plays frequently include dance as an essential ingredient of the plot – for example, *Dancing at Lughnasa*, *Stepping Out* – or in a climatic moment such as in *Stones In His Pockets*. Without great physical control you could not be cast in a play such as *Up 'N Under* with its fantastic rugby sequence. Pantomimes, children's shows and music hall require an ability to perform simple steps. A short sequence of ballroom dancing occurs in many plays and in period drama, and even if no historic dance as such is included, a knowledge of it is extremely helpful in achieving the correct style and carriage of your body. So, in these days of increased competition for every part, the more ability you can have in the field of dance, the more your employment potential increases.

You need to know your own body too, and know what is the best way to warm it up for the performance ahead. Any training will help, even aerobics or "keep fit" classes should help stamina and movement. However, it is better to learn a basic discipline and, if you took lessons as a child, to build on and consolidate this. Local dance schools frequently have general classes in tap and ballet for older students, and although ballet might sound daunting it is good for control and basic steps. There are evening classes, societies and clubs for just about everything . . . flamenco, jive, folk dancing (a good source of basic steps), Irish, Scottish, historical dance and increasingly various styles of Indian dance. The more you learn the easier it will be to "pick up" and perform sequences in auditions and then, having got the part, in a production!'

The City Literary Institute in London offers classes in a wide range of performance skills, such as mime, improvisation, singing, dancing, playing musical instruments and *sometimes* even juggling, at very reasonable fees. And it is worthwhile finding out if your local council has anything to offer in the way of drama workshops and tuition.

more about auditioning

ANJI CARROLL trained as an actress at the Bristol Old Vic School before side-stepping into casting some ten years later. Having served four years' apprenticeship as Casting Assistant to Di Carling, where she worked on projects like *This Life*, Anji decided to become a casting director in her own right. Over the last three years, among other things, Anji has been Casting Director on *The Bill*, a children's series for Granada, two series of *London's Burning* and the 'Half Hour' plays for Channel 4:

'When adults are making the transition from "child actor" to "grown up" there is an all-important question to be asked: "Is this *really* what I want to be doing now I'm an adult?" The grim truth of the matter is that work opportunities are minimal, and even if you've been successful as a child your good fortune may not continue. Unless you are absolutely 100% sure you want to pursue this career – don't!

If you *are* sure, the next question to ask is should you go to drama school? And if so, where? When? You may feel you can make the transition more easily if you do. Others, especially those of you who have attended full-time theatre schools, may benefit from going later, after a few years in the business. Either way, I am a great advocate of drama school training. I went at 18 and had the best three years ever. However, the process of trying to get there can be slow and undoubtedly expensive. If drama school is the way forwards for you my advice is to apply for as many as possible. The courses and the way in which they are run vary tremendously: by visiting half a dozen or more you will have a clearer idea, not only of what's available where, but of which school's training appeals most to you.

Making the transition is not just a matter of years but also of maturity. Auditioners and fellow actors alike will now expect a little extra commitment/dedication. This shouldn't be a horrifying awakening as it only means one fundamental, yet often overlooked, thing – listening. At Bristol it was suggested to us that "acting" is inaccurately named and that it should really be called "reacting" or "interacting". *Always listen.* By listening to thoughts on the project, character, scene/s, the spoken word and so on you will be able to react in an informed way.

If you are expected to learn a speech for an audition, choose something that is near to you in age and experience and be sure you have learnt it word for word. Get to your audition early – especially if you have reading difficulties and there are scenes to look at. If you have been sent a script beforehand read all of it, not just your part. If you are reading a scene, listen and react with the person/s reading alongside you – probably us, the auditioners, who aren't necessarily Oliviers, though we do try! Remember not to hide your face and look up wherever possible. Never be under-prepared. Be confident but not cocky. And remember: *all* auditioners want auditionees to do well. They're on your side. Don't let them or yourself down.

. . . And finally, *don't forget to enjoy!*'

GABRIELLE DAWES is Deputy Casting Director at the National Theatre, where she has cast over thirty productions, and has been involved in the casting of numerous others. Recent freelance casting includes: *Philip Pullman's Aladdin* (Bristol Old Vic), *Hello & Goodbye* (ETT), *Gizmo Love* (ATC). Television: *Elmina's Kitchen* (BBC). Film: *Perdie* (BAFTA-nominated, Best Short Film); *The Suicide Club*.

'You will probably find that each auditioning experience will be different, to a greater or lesser extent, depending on the Director's preferred working practices and the nature of the piece you are auditioning for. You can significantly increase your chances of doing a good audition by being as prepared as possible, and you can do this by acquiring a range of skills, material and information.

Some directors prefer actors to do speeches at auditions, so it is certainly a good idea to have three or four contrasting pieces, classical and modern, in your repertoire. Choose pieces that you feel play to your strengths, giving you the opportunity to show what you can do well.

However, you are just as likely to be asked to read a passage from the play that you are auditioning for. Usually the Casting Director will send you the script in advance: if not, go out and buy a copy (if it's published) or, as a last resort, ask if you can arrive early to look at the script before going in. In any event, don't go into an audition not having read the whole script at least once. You want the Director to think you're interested and informed, as well as talented, and there are few things more embarrassing and time-wasting than an actor who is obviously unprepared.

Practise your sight-reading skills as well, for those times where the Director asks you to look at a different or additional passage to the one you've prepared. Lots of people find sight-reading quite difficult, so help yourself by picking up any book, opening it at a random page and reading it out aloud without scanning it first. Practise this exercise often, with a different passage each time, and you'll acquire a confidence with sight-reading that could one day make the difference between getting or not getting a job.

And if you are dyslexic, do let the Casting Director know at the point of setting up the audition. They will then be aware that it would help to get the script to you as much in advance of the audition as possible, to give you plenty of time to prepare.

The key thing to remember about auditions is that we want you to get the job! So turn up in good time, knowing all about what you're being sent for, and as prepared as possible in view of the information you or your agent has been given by the Casting Director. Listen to what the Director asks you, and try to relax and enjoy the audition enough to show a glimpse of the real you – the aspects of your talent and personality that makes you irresistible for the job!'

out on your own

Once you've left the safety of stage or drama school and you're 'on your own', the grim prospect of looking for work looms up – as it does for lots of other students leaving schools, colleges and universities. Auditions can be few and far between and you owe it to yourself to make the most of every opportunity. Some people do really well at drama school, are given a leading role in the final showcase and find themselves a good agent before they've even completed their course. Others are not so fortunate. One graduate told me he was given the part of a 60-year-old 'Butler' in his final show, and what was the use of that! The old saying, 'There are no small parts, only small actors' was not much consolation. And agents or casting directors are more likely to take notice of the actor playing a reasonable part in his or her own age group (although it must be said that playing an 'elderly part', if it's done really well, can be both intriguing to the onlooker and satisfying for the actor).

A sub-editor working for a national newspaper said her Editor once told them that often, the most brilliant students at university did very little after they'd left. It was the ones who were aware that they were not as bright or as beautiful as their contemporaries that did the best in the long run. They tried that much harder!

Many young actors today find work in children's or young people's theatre. A friend of mine played 'Edmund' in a tour of *The Lion, the Witch and the Wardrobe* when he first left drama school – and he was 24 at the time! A lot of thought and care goes into these productions and not only can you learn a lot from them, you are also helping to encourage new audiences for the future.

ALAN AYCKBOURN – Artistic Director of the Stephen Joseph Theatre, Scarborough, and one of our busiest and most popular playwrights and directors. has this to say about the importance of working in children's theatre:

'I immensely enjoy writing plays for children, or really what I prefer to call the "family" audience, because it's probably as hard if not harder than writing for adults. You have to be more aware. Children won't lie to you – they judge you immediately. They can get bored very quickly. Adults are polite people normally and if something is a little boring, they'll sit and watch it and think, "Well, it'll get more interesting in a minute." But children just go, "Boring" and turn round and talk to their friends. All the things that matter in any sort of theatre matter twice as much for children. Good story, good dialogue, characters you are interested in. My imagination really catches fire sometimes! To write for such an audience sharpens your playwriting skills no end. It's affected my adult work, I know. In fact, one such play, *Wildest Dreams* – a quite frightening play – is in one sense entirely a children's play. I'd never have written it if I hadn't experienced the thrills and spills of writing for the younger audience.

The shame in this country, of course, is how little importance is attached to children's theatre. It's appallingly underfunded – the companies that do exist providing quality work all year round survive on a shoestring. There are many excellent writers producing scripts for children but there should be many more. But how can there be when they receive precious little monetary reward and hardly any critical acknowledgement?

Young people are the theatregoers of tomorrow, but if they're never given the chance to see exciting, innovative and imaginative theatre in their childhood, how can they develop an interest in watching plays in their adulthood? If we're not careful, they will be lost forever to television, cinema and all those special effects. They will never have experienced the joy of watching something 'handmade' especially for them in one particular place on one particular day. That's what the "liveness: of theatre is about and what we have got to keep alive.'

VICKY IRELAND – playwright and, until recently, Artistic Director of the Polka Theatre for Children, has this to say about auditioning and working for children's theatre:

'When we present theatre for young audiences we demand exactly the same production values as for "adult theatre", so we're looking for excellence in all departments. At the same time, ours is a specialised field of work which expects commitment and respect. We are fiercely proud, so don't arrive with a patronising attitude.

One group we frequently need to portray are children and teenagers, so young actors are often cast. You don't have to "act" being a child, just carry the spirit inside you and let it inform your behaviour. Don't worry, we call upon a whole range of actors so there are lots of other characters you can try for.

Most children's theatre is physically demanding so you need to be really fit and have plenty of stamina. And, because children's audiences can behave in unexpected ways, you must have a real sense of humour and be light on your feet in order to adjust. We are also looking for generosity of spirit – you may well have to be with a small group for some time in testing circumstances.

If you get an audition, the following tips might help you.

- If possible, acquire some knowledge of the company's work before the audition.
- If the play is published you should read it, but as most of our work is new writing, you may not get the chance.
- If you don't have an agent, ask as many questions as you need to before the audition. The basics are: details of character, dates, where performing and money.
- Always be sure to note clearly the address of the audition place, the name of who you'll be meeting and a contact phone number.
- Work out carefully how long it will take to get to where you're going, and always arrive in good time. If you are running late, ring to explain. Don't arrive in a sweat; this might be interpreted as being unfit. Take your time, go to the loo, have a drink of water, etc. Then read the piece of script carefully. Better to get your focus than rush in and feel unready.
- If you're not a good sight-reader, say so. Any auditioner will allow for this.
- Be well turned out. Children's theatre is usually physical, so don't wear high-heeled boots or tight jeans, gorgeous as they may be. Better to wear smart, clean clothes you can move in easily.
- Remember bodily hygiene. Use deodorant.
- Don't drink alcohol just before your audition or reek of tobacco smoke. It's a turn-off.
- It is vital to have prepared a speech or speeches. Choose a good audition piece that suits you and that you feel happy and comfortable with, not a hastily cobbled piece of children's literature. Remember, we are looking for good actors. We don't judge the piece, rather the performer, and we can cope with four-letter words if there are some in the piece you want to do.
- Have a song ready to sing, just in case – with or without accompaniment.
- Being able to play a musical instrument is an asset.
- Be prepared to improvise.
- Be prepared to do and give more than you expect. If you aren't right for what you've gone for, you might be asked to do something unrelated, to do with a part in the future. Just go with it.

Remember: energy, focus, sense of humour and commitment. Play from the heart and good luck.'

JONATHON SIDDALL – Artistic Director Education, Hampstead Theatre:

'"Just Do It" used to be an advertising slogan for a make of trainer, and it's great advice for anybody wanting to develop their skills and move into a performing career.

The extracts contained in this book are really the starting point. When you have found one that suits you, try it out. If you are at school or college, you have facilities to showcase the monologues; indeed, you have a ready audience made up of friends and fellow students. Approach your tutors, ask for direction and put yourself on the line. Plays are written to be performed, and only by performing them can you gauge your abilities and the effect of your acting.

If you have no facilities or are not at school or college, the next step is your local theatre. Nowadays most companies run their own youth groups with regular performances at their theatres. These groups are an ideal forum for developing your skills – they usually have strong links with theatre professionals and you'll find yourself working with technicians, designers, actors and directors who all have professional experience. At Hampstead Theatre you can perform in new plays written by specially commissioned writers. Adults can also find a number of adult groups linked to others offering similar opportunities.

When you are in a production, invite your teachers; invite your local theatre and get your face known. After all, the only way people will think of you for the next show is if they have seen you perform.

At the end of the day the experience of creating and performing theatre can not be separated from these monologues – they are all parts of plays. So find an audience to perform them to – even younger brothers or sisters. Pick the monologue that suits you and then read the full script so that when you perform it, you will have a better ability to really understand the subtext. Whom is your character talking to? Do they believe in what they are saying? What do they want the effect of their words to be? Remember, you are an actor and the audience comes to see and hear the subtext. If they didn't want that, they could sit at home, read this book and never set foot inside the theatre!'

advice from the actors

Pat Keen played the 'Sergeant' in the original production of *The Passing-Out Parade* (*see* page 98) which opened at Greenwich Theatre in September 1979. She has had a long career in theatre, with roles from 'Margaret More' in *A Man For All Seasons* at the Globe Theatre (now called the Gielgud) to the 'Mrs Squeers'/'Mrs Crummles' double in the Royal Shakespeare Company's *Nicholas Nickleby* tour, starting at Stratford on Avon and going to the States. Her film roles have included John Schlesinger's *A Kind of Loving*, a Sherlock Holmes spoof *Without A Clue* with Michael Caine, and *Clockwise* with John Cleese. She has also worked with John Cleese in the TV series *Fawlty Towers*, and played 'Addy' in the TV series *Down to Earth*. Here she emphasises the importance of reading the whole play:

'It was World War Two. I was eight. It was summer and I was sitting on a gate by the road when I heard shouting. Suddenly two girls in ATS uniform riding bikes and pedalling furiously shot down the road screaming with laughter and shouting ribald remarks to each other. The one in front threw all caution to the winds as she steered with one hand and turned back to shout at her friend. This glimpse showed a "devil may care" attitude freed from the restraint of how "nice" girls should behave.

If you choose this extract, it's important to read the whole play because that "devil may care" attitude runs through it. Besides being very amusing it also shows how it affects "Stokes" – what she does and how others treat her.

I thoroughly enjoyed playing the "Sergeant" and when I first joined the cast we were all taken to a place that made uniforms. Anne Valery, the author, had been in the ATS and was insistent that we should have the right material. She crawled over huge bolts 12 feet wide trying to find the exact stuff, rejecting one after another until with a triumphant "This is it!" she recognised a particularly spiky and scratchy khaki wool. Later in the dress rehearsals we had to get used to the weight plus shirt, bloomers, thick stockings, overcoat, gas cape, gas mask and tin helmet and the heavy ATS-issue leather shoes. On the first night I was standing in the wings wearing all this clobber except for the gas cape, mask and helmet waiting for the curtain call. The scene-dock door at the Greenwich Theatre was open and I saw what I thought was a heavy mist coming in from the park. Then I realised that it was coming from me. It was just as Anne had told us happened after route marches: I was steaming like a horse!'

MICHAEL CONRAD trained at Rose Bruford College of Speech and Drama, graduating in 1994. His very first job was playing four contrasting parts in *The Queen and I* at the Vaudeville Theatre, London, followed by a national tour. He has since appeared in various roles for both TV and theatre, most notably in the highly acclaimed play *Talking About Men* at the Oval House. On television he has appeared in *The Bill*, *Rumble* and *The Incredible Sock Monster*. He is also appearing in a series of adverts for 'Oasis', the fruit drink:

'I think it is imperative that anyone entering the profession of acting these days should try and acquire a *second* profession. Acting is a fantastic job but there will be periods of unemployment. This can be both frustrating and soul-destroying. Before I became an actor, I trained as a decorator, so when I am not acting I can fall back on my earlier profession. I also think it gives one a certain grounding and stability which is not necessarily found in this precarious business.

Auditions can be quite a daunting and intimidating experience at the beginning. But the more you audition the better you become at them. Once you become comfortable with them they can be enjoyable – even exciting. Always try to find out as much information as possible about your character, the play and the playwright. If you are auditioning for a play, make sure that you read it beforehand. If you can't get hold of a copy, go to the library. You need to be prepared for the audition and this will give you greater understanding and confidence. If there is no copy available, try to get to the appointment at least 30 minutes before the start to familiarise yourself with the script.

Never go to an audition unprepared! It is very unprofessional. A director may also ask you to improvise or read another character – so be ready! It is also a very good idea to have at least three speeches in your repertoire as some auditioners may require you to perform something. Try to have contrasting speeches to show your range. And never, ever do an accent that you cannot master – it is very embarrassing watching an actor who cannot do the accent required, and you won't be doing yourself any favours.

Don't get disheartened if you don't get the job, it may be due to a number of factors – perhaps you are too tall, or too short, or the wrong age – so never take it personally. Believe in yourself and others will believe in you.'

REBECCA CALLARD played 'Arietty' in the children's television serial *The Borrowers* when she was 17, and 'Juliet' in Judi Dench's production of *Romeo and Juliet* for the New Shakespeare Company at the Regent's Park Open Air Theatre. She has since graduated to adult roles, playing 'Kate' in the Granada Television serial *The Grand*, for which she was nominated for two 'Best Actress Awards', and the tour representative 'Laura' in the BBC Television series *Sunburn* set in Cyprus and later in Portugal. She recently returned to the New Shakespeare Company to play 'Hermia' in *A Midsummer Night's Dream*:

'I've always wanted to be an actress, ever since I can remember. It's in my blood, I think. I fell into it when I was young, and now I look back I can't believe how lucky I was. It was so easy to get an Equity card back then and before I knew it I was going from job to job.

When you're young you don't get nerves because it's not the end of the world if you don't get a job. But as you get older there seem to be more and more talented actresses and less and less work. I've been fortunate enough to be pretty much constantly working. I don't know why or how, I really think it is just luck. I can't remember ever having a bad audition or being truly nervous before I was 18. But then, once I started to want jobs so badly, I'd have to concentrate on keeping control and focusing. At 19, 20 I still looked 15 so when I auditioned for parts of my own age invariably it didn't work out. Which knocks your confidence. But then as you get older you realise there are all sorts of reasons why you might get rejected. (And it really does seem like rejection.) You might be too small, too tall, too blonde or too brunette or even too young-looking! All these things can make you feel like a failure. But you're not, and you must turn those feelings around and become stronger. It really can be something about your appearance that stops you getting a job. So I believe that you must do one hundred percent the best audition you can do, and then if you don't get it you can't blame yourself.

If I get pages or a script for television or film early enough, I will learn the lines. They tend to tape most auditions now so looking down at the page won't show your face or eyes. Obviously if you get the script just before you go in, go through it as many times as you can.

With theatre I first read the whole play, and then read the scenes out loud over and over again until I'm familiar enough with the lines to be ready to move them around if the director wants to. I work really hard on auditions and lock myself away for days. If I don't get the part I've conditioned myself to move on to the next. And at least I know I worked as hard as I could.

I look at it this way: if I'm out of work, auditions are my only chance to act. And that's all I can do, really!'

a word about the speeches

Each of the following speeches has its own introduction, giving the date of the original production – information often required for auditions and drama examinations – a few lines about the play itself and the scene leading up to the actual speech. Even so, it is important to read the *whole* play. Not only are you likely to be asked questions, such as 'What happened in the previous scene?', but the other characters in the play can also give you vital information about your own character.

At the top left corner of each introduction I have – where possible – given the age or approximate age of the character, together with their nationality and/or the region or area they come from. If a region or nationality is not mentioned then standard English, RP (Received Pronunciation) or your own normal voice should be used.

Some characters, such as Frankie in *Member of the Wedding* and Carl in *Madame Melville* are very young. But these are leading parts and are played on stage by older and more experienced actors, usually in their early twenties. They are, however, excellent speeches for young actors and students in the '16 plus' group as well as even younger actors for both auditions and drama examinations.

choosing a speech

Make sure you read audition requirements carefully, particularly with regard to your classical speech. The classical speeches in this book are from plays written in the following periods:

Elizabethan (1558–1603)
Romeo and Juliet and *A Midsummer Night's Dream*
Jacobean (1603–1625)
The Witch of Edmonton
Late Eighteenth Century
The Rivals and *She Stoops To Conquer*
Late Nineteenth Century
An Ideal Husband
Early Twentieth Century
Fanny's First Play and *Back to Methuselah*

Shakespeare's plays

The speeches used here from *A Midsummer Night's Dream* and *Romeo and Juliet* are all written in blank verse. A speech from Shakespeare or another Elizabethan/Jacobean play is usually one of the requirements for auditioning for full-time drama school, and also for drama exams at the Guildhall School of Music and Drama and the London Academy of Music and Drama (LAMDA).

Professional theatre companies like the Royal Shakespeare, the Royal National Theatre, the New Shakespeare Company at Regent's Park, the marvellous London Bubble Theatre and the various Open Air Theatre companies producing Shakespeare up and down the country also expect you to be able to cope with blank verse.

So it can be a useful source of work for those that take the trouble to learn to do it well!

Blank verse is verse that does not rhyme, but has a recognisable rhythm. Fortunately, the rhythm used by Shakespeare and by most playwrights in this period is the one we use now in everyday speech. It is the measure, pulse or pattern most natural to the English Language: an unstressed syllable followed by stressed syllable. When actors understand this, they find speaking blank verse very much easier than they thought, and realise they don't need to declaim it in tortured tones or stand up and recite it like a poem. These speeches come from plays, and plays are meant to be acted.

There are many instances in blank verse where there is no punctuation at the end of a line and you need to read straight on to the next line to make the speech make sense. For example, in Juliet's speech from *Romeo and Juliet*, the lines:

Now is the sun upon the highmost hill
Of this day's journey, and from nine to twelve
Is three long hours, yet she is not come . . .

If you take a great breath after 'highmost hill' and again after 'twelve' the speech will be choppy and will not make good sense. Similarly Romeo's speech:

More honourable state, more courtship lives
In carrion flies than Romeo. They may seize
On the white wonder of dear Juliet's hand
And steal immortal blessing from her lips . . .

A breath taken after 'lives' and 'seize' would spoil both the sense and the language and it would not be easily understood.

Most people agree that you should not take a breath at the end of a line where the sense runs on, but there are of course exceptions to this rule – depending sometimes on a particular characterisation or mood, and often in a production, or the Director's own ideas on the subject. But at an audition or drama examination I think it's best to be on the safe side!

VALERIE KING BA (Hons) Cert Ed, LLAM (Hons), LGSM; Head of Drama at Laine Theatre Arts and Examiner for the London Academy of Music and Dramatic Art (LAMDA) has this to say:

'The author's eclectic choice of stimulating and challenging scenes will surely inspire young performers.

Jean Marlow presents a range of literature from different periods and cultures. These scenes are varied in subject, tone, mood, language and style. The useful introductions help to set the scene in context and provide valuable background information.

These innovative and carefully researched scenes are eminently suitable for auditions, examinations and festivals, enabling young actors to present a broad and balanced programme well suited to their artistic capabilities and talents.'

audition speeches
for men

Wint Selby – American, aged 19

AH! WILDERNESS EUGENE O'NEILL

First performed at the Nixon Theatre, Pittsburgh, Pennsylvania, in 1933 and transferred in the same year to the Guild Theatre, New York. It is a comedy set in 1906 and described as a study of middle-class family life.

Nat Miller, owner of *The Evening Globe*, lives in Connecticut with his wife and four children – Arthur, the eldest who is at Yale, 16-year-old Richard, and young Mildred and Tommy. It is the Fourth of July and the family are at dinner. Richard's girlfriend has left him and he is feeling wretched. His mother tells him it is his own fault. Upset, he walks out of the dining room.

Outside he hears a low whistle coming from the porch. It is **Wint Selby**, a classmate of Arthur's at Yale and a typical college boy of the period. He has called to see Arthur but he is out. He explains to Richard that he has dated a couple of girls for the night, but cannot afford to buy drinks for both of them. The situation is urgent. Richard offers to lend him 11 dollars. But **Wint** doesn't want his money, he wants Richard to stand in for his elder brother.

Published by Jonathan Cape, London

Wint

(As he enters - warningly, in a low tone) Keep it quiet, Kid. I don't want the folks to know I'm here. Tell Art I want to see him a second – on the QT . . . *(irritably)* Damn! I thought he'd be here for dinner. *(More irritably)* Hell, that gums the works for fair! . . . I ran into a couple of swift babies from New Haven this after, and I dated them up for tonight, thinking I could catch Art. But now it's too late to get anyone else and I'll have to pass it up. I'm nearly broke and I can't afford to blow them both to drinks . . . *(shaking his head)* Nix, Kid, I don't want to borrow your money. *(Then getting an idea)* But say, have you got anything on for tonight?. . . Want to come along with me? *(Then quickly)* I'm not trying to lead you astray, understand. But it'll be a help if you would just sit around with Belle and feed her a few drinks while I'm off with Edith. *(He winks)* See what I mean? You don't have to do anything, not even take a glass of beer – unless you want to . . . Ever been out with any girls– I mean, real swift ones that there's something doing with, not these dead Janes around here . . . Ever drink anything besides sodas? . . . *(impressed)* Hell, you know more than I thought. *(Then considering)* Can you fix it so your folks won't get wise? I don't want your old man coming after me. You can get back by half-past ten or eleven, though, all right. Think you can cook up some lie to cover that? *(As Richard hesitates - encouraging him)* Ought to be easy – on the Fourth . . . But you've got to keep your face closed about this, you hear? – to Art and everybody else. I tell you straight, I wouldn't ask you to come if I wasn't in a hole – and if I didn't know you were coming down to Yale next year, and didn't think you're giving me the straight goods about having been around before. I don't want to lead you astray . . . Well, you be at the Pleasant Beach Hotel at half-past nine then. Come in the back room. And don't forget to grab some cloves to take the booze off your breath . . . See you later, then. *(He starts out and is just about to close the door when he thinks of something)* And say, I'll say you're a Harvard freshman, and you back me up. They don't know a damn thing about Harvard. I don't want them thinking I'm travelling around with any high-school kid . . . So long then. You better beat it right after your dinner while you've got a chance, and hang around until it's time. Watch your step, Kid.

Guy Bennett – aged 17

ANOTHER COUNTRY JULIAN MITCHELL

First produced at the Greenwich Theatre in 1981, then transferred to the Queens Theatre, London, and revived at The Arts Theatre, London, in 2000.

The play takes place in an English public school in the early 30s, where future leaders of the ruling class are being prepared for their entry into the Establishment. In this environment the two central characters – **Guy Bennett**, coming to terms with his homosexuality, and Tommy Judd, a committed Marxist – are very much 'outsiders'.

In this scene, set in the fourth-year library, **Bennett**, Judd and Devenish are talking about the Dedication they have just attended. Judd dismisses it as ludicrous for 400 boys to line up and blub for a lot of people they never knew who died in a businessman's war. **Bennet** remarks that it made him think of his father whom he loathed, and goes on to describe in detail the ghastly circumstances of his death.

Published by Amber Lane Press

Bennett

It was the Easter hols. I was reading in bed one night when I heard the most peculiar noise – a sort of muffled squeaking. I thought it was the cat at first. But then it went on and on – sort of feeble and desperate at the same time. Like something trapped. So I got up and looked out into the passage. It seemed to be coming from my parents' room, and there was a light under the door, so I assumed – well, I mean, what would you have thought? . . . I was just going back to bed to mind my own business, and feeling pretty queasy because – well, I mean, one's own parents! . . . When I quite distinctly heard my mater say, 'Help!' *(He imitates her)* 'Help!' *(Devenish is enthralled. Judd is more and more sceptical)* It was terribly eerie. Complete silence, then suddenly there it was again. 'Help!' So – I didn't know what to do. I went down the passage to their door. I listened a moment, then I knocked and said, 'Are you all right?' And she said – *(Imitation of the muffled voice again)* – 'Guy! Quick – help!' She sounded absolutely at her last gasp. So I turned the door handle to go in – only of course the door was locked . . . All the bedroom keys are the same in our house. I see why now. But it took me ages to push their key out backwards and get mine in. And then, when I finally got the door open – my pater had had a heart attack right in the middle of – *(Judd claps ironically, Bennett turns on him)* Have you ever tried lifting your father's corpse off your living mother? . . . It's incredibly difficult. He was like a huge sack of – of wet mud. The weight never went where I was expecting . . . My mother kept her eyes shut the whole time. I suppose she thought if she couldn't see me, I couldn't see her. But of course I could . . . He was a very fleshy man. And they were in rather a complicated position. I think that's what did it. The mechanics were too much for him. There was a ghastly moment I thought I might have to break one of his arms . . . What made it all the more macabre was, I'd always hated him. He was a complete loather. Whereas my mother – I couldn't help thinking – it's all right for him – what better way to go? But for *her* – and *me*, seeing her, like it says in the Bible, uncovered – I honestly wondered if we'd ever be able to look each other in the eye again. If you ask me, it's why she's marrying this awful Colonel person.

Serpent

BACK TO METHUSELAH
GEORGE BERNARD SHAW

First presented by the Theatre Guild at the Garrick Theatre, New York, in 1922. In his preface Shaw says that he has written this play as a contribution to the modern Bible.

In this first section – 'In The Beginning' – Adam and Eve are in the Garden of Eden and, curled around the branches of a great tree, is an immense **Serpent**. Adam has discovered a fawn lying with its neck broken. He calls to Eve and together they try to revive the creature. It is their first experience of death and they are very frightened. As Adam goes off to throw the fawn's body into the river, the **Serpent** becomes visible, glowing in wonderful new colours. It rears its head slowly and speaks seductively into Eve's ear.

Published by Penguin Books, London

Serpent

Eve . . . It was I who whispered the word to you that you did not know.
Dead. Death. Die . . . Death is not an unhappy thing when you have
learnt how to conquer it . . . By another thing, called birth . . . The
serpent never dies. Some day you shall see me come out of this beautiful skin, a new snake with a new and lovelier skin. That is birth . . . If I
can do that, what can I not do? I tell you I am very subtle. When you
and Adam talk, I hear you say 'Why?' Always 'Why?' You see things;
and you say 'Why?' But I dream things that never were; and I say 'Why
not?' . . . Why not be born again and again as I am, new and beautiful
every time? . . . Listen. I will tell you a great secret. I am very subtle;
and I have thought and thought and thought. And I am very wilful, and
must have what I want; and I have willed and willed and willed. And I
have eaten strange things: stones and apples that you are afraid to eat . . .
I dared everything . . . I gathered a part of the life in my body, and shut
it into a tiny white case made of the stones I had eaten . . . I shewed
the little case to the sun, and left it in its warmth. And it burst; and a
little snake came out; and it became bigger and bigger from day to day
until it was as big as I. That was the second birth . . . It nearly tore me
asunder. Yet I am alive, and can burst my skin and renew myself as before.
Soon there will be as many snakes in Eden as there are scales on my
body. Then death will not matter: this snake and that snake will die; but
the snakes will live . . . Think. Will. Eat the dust. Lick the white stone:
bite the apple you dread. The sun will give life . . . Do. Dare it. Everything
is possible: everything.

eddie - young, American

A BRIEF HISTORY OF HELEN OF TROY
OR EVERYTHING WILL BE DIFFERENT
MARK SCHULTZ

Originally produced in the US by the Soho Repertory Theatre and first performed in the UK at the Drum Theatre, Plymouth in 2005.

Charlotte is grief-stricken by the death of her beautiful mother. She is obsessed by Helen of Troy and her fantasies of becoming an object of desire start to spill over into normal life.

Freddie is every young girl's ideal lover. Tall and handsome, he has no time for Charlotte and tells her to stop pestering her.

In this fantasy scene, Charlotte is lying on her bed as **Freddie** enters her bedroom. He is bare-chested and is carrying a football. He has come to confess his love for her.

Published by Oberon Modern Plays, London
The full text is currently available from Oberon Books, ISBN: 1840026340.

Freddie

Um. Hi.

Charlotte.

Um.

Okay I know this is awkward and everything. Me just coming here and all. Like this. I mean I know I just really met you and everything. But I've seen you. Really. And I just gotta. I had to come and tell you. You know. And.

This is embarrassing, I know. And I don't mean it to be. It's not supposed to be. I mean. But. Jesus, it's cold out, right? Anyway there's like a million things I wanna tell you right now, Charlotte. And I just. I don't know. Like. You have such a cool room. I really like your bedspread.

Um.

This is usually the other way around.

Okay I've seen you. And. You are so. Pretty. I think. I mean. I think you're pretty. Right. Um. So I'll just come out and say it. Okay. I think I love you. Charlotte. I really do. And. It's not like this happens every day. You know. For me. I don't just like fall in love with people. It's hard. And I've really fallen for you. And I know it's stupid and like. Stupid and everything. But. I wanna know if maybe we can go out and be like boyfriend girlfriend or something I don't know. 'Cause I'm really. I'm. In love. With you. And it's hard. Keeping it inside. All the time. And I came here to say that. And ask you. You know. If we can maybe. Go out sometime. And. Eat something. Or. Watch a movie. Or I don't know. I got a great entertainment system at home. I could show you. DVD. Surround sound and everything. It's really cool. But. You know.

We could go out and. Maybe I could touch you. And. Maybe you'd let me kiss you. I mean if that's okay. Is that okay? 'Cause I really love you. I really wanna be with you. It's so important to me right now. I really. Just had to come and tell you. I couldn't wait. Um.

Shit I gotta get back to practice. Um.

Okay. I love you. Please love me.

Oh. And. I'm really sorry. About your mom. Being dead and all. That sucks.

I gotta go.

Morgan Evans – Welsh, aged 17

THE CORN IS GREEN EMLYN WILLIAMS

First produced at the Duchess Theatre, London, in 1938 and set in a mining village in the Welsh countryside in the late 1800s.

An English teacher, Miss Moffat, comes down from London to take over the house left to her by her uncle. There is an old barn next door and she decides to turn it into a school for the local children. One of her pupils – a young miner, **Morgan Evans** – shows exceptional promise and for the next two years she takes a special interest in him, eventually persuading the local squire to fund his application for a scholarship to Oxford.

In this scene **Morgan** has begun to resent his studies and, unknown to Miss Moffat, has been drinking every evening in the Gwesmor Arms with the local lads. Miss Moffat tells him she has entered him for the scholarship and is going to start teaching him Greek. She has also found him a nail-file and will show him how to use it. **Morgan** flings his pen down on the table and announces that he is going back to the coal-mine.

Published by Heinemann Educational Books, Oxford

Morgan

(Quietly) I shall not need a nail-file in the coal-mine . . . I am going back to the coal-mine . . . *(She turns and looks at him. He rises, breathing fast. They look at each other. A pause)* I do not want to learn Greek, nor to pronounce any long English words, nor to keep my hands clean . . . Because . . . *(plunging)* . . . because I was born in a Welsh hayfield when my mother was helpin' with the harvest – and I always lived in a little house with no stairs only a ladder – and no water – and until my brothers was killed I never sleep except three in a bed. I know that is terrible grammar but it is true . . . The last two years I have not had no proper talk with English chaps in the mine because I was so busy keepin' this old grammar in its place. Tryin' to better myself . . . *(his voice rising . . .* tryin' to better myself, the day and the night! . . . You cannot take a nail-file into the Gwesmor Arms public bar! . . . I have been there every afternoon for a week, spendin' your pocket-money, and I have been there now, and that is why I can speak my mind! . . . Because you are not interested in me . . . *(losing control)* How can you be interested in a machine that you put a penny in and if nothing comes out you give it a good shake? 'Evans, write me an essay, Evans, get up and bow, Evans, what is a subjunctive!' My name is Morgan Evans, and all my friends call me Morgan, and if there is anything gets on the wrong side of me it is callin' me Evans! . . . And do you know what they call me in the village? Ci bach yr ysgol! The schoolmistress's little dog. What has it got to do with you if my nails are dirty? Mind your own business! *(He bursts into sobs and buries his head in his hands on the end of the sofa.)*

Honey – aged 18

CRESSIDA NICHOLAS WRIGHT

First produced by the Almeida Theatre at the Albery Theatre, London, in March 2000.

Actor and talent scout John Shank is a trainer of boy players in the London theatre of the 1630s. He has foolishly invested in Master Gunnell's theatre, but Gunnell has disappeared and Shank is on the edge of financial ruin. Before he left, Gunnell sent him a new boy, Stephen Hammerton, who begged Shank to train him as an actor, but now it seems he will have to be sold.

It is late at night and Stephen, together with an older boy, **Honey**, has crept through the trap door into the costume store of Master Gunnell's theatre. It appears to be stripped bare, but behind the curtains are some expensive gowns. If they can take these back to Shank he can pay off his debts and Stephen won't have to be sold after all.

In this scene **Honey** has tried on one of the gowns and is smoking a pipe. Stephen has always admired **Honey**, who is extremely experienced and one of Shank's most talented and successful young players. Stephen asks him to explain about acting. Is it all just 'a matter of standing straight and saying your lines'?

Published by Nick Hern Books, London

Honey

It's different at different times . . . When you're young, you're just a child being clever. Then it changes . . . When you get older. When other boys get tall and clumsy. And their voices drop two million pegs. We don't do that. We hang on . . . It's like a baby falling down a well. You've got its foot in your hand and you don't let go. So you're not one thing exactly. You're half man, half boy. That's when you find you can really do it. And it's amazing. It's better than beer or wine. It's better than smoking. It's like flying. It's like finding that wings have suddenly sprouted from your shoulders. You come on stage and everything happens the way it's meant to. And nobody in the audience looks at anyone else. Because you live in a sort of stolen time that they can't get to. Except through you. And it could disappear at any moment. You're like a soldier on the eve of battle. Every night could be your last. And everyone wants to be that special person on that special night. That's my theory. That's why they grab old Jhon, J, H, O, N, and give him notes for us. It's why they hang about at the Actors' Door. *(He puts out the pipe, starts getting out of his dress)* I still get letters every day. Not just from men. Everyone thinks I'm just a boyish bugger. That's not true. I see women as well. They're even stranger than the men are. They ask me to supper and want me to bring my gown and make-up. *(He stands, the gown in his arms)* Take it. *(Stephen takes it. Honey gets the other gowns)* We'll carry them back to Shanky. He'll pay his debt to the Board and you'll stay on. Isn't that what you wanted?

Jhon an old theatre dresser at the Globe

Billy – West of Ireland, aged 17–18

THE CRIPPLE OF INISHMAAN
MARTIN MCDONAGH

First performed at the Cottesloe auditorium of the Royal National Theatre in 1996 and set on a remote island off the west coast of Ireland in 1934.

A Hollywood film director has arrived on the neighbouring Island of Inishmore to film *Man of Aran* and young cripple **Billy** is determined to get a part. Pretending to have contracted TB, he produces a supposed letter from the doctor saying he hasn't much longer to live and persuades local fisherman Babbybobby, whose wife had recently died of the disease, to take him across to Inishmore on his boat. There is a part for a cripple boy in the film and **Billy** is taken to Hollywood to test for the role. The test turns out to be a complete failure and **Billy** returns to Inishmaan, shamed by his experience.

In this scene he apologises to Bobbybabby for 'codding' him along and attempts to explain what has happened. Bobby's reply is to pick up a length of lead piping and knock him to the ground.

Published by Methuen Drama

Billy

Babbybobby. I daresay I owe you an explanation . . . I want to, Bobby. See, I never thought at all this day would come when I'd have to explain. I'd hoped I'd disappear forever to America. And I would've too, if they'd wanted me there. If they'd wanted me for the filming. But they didn't want me. A blond lad from Fort Lauderdale they hired instead of me. He wasn't crippled at all, but the Yank said, 'Ah, better to get a normal fella who can act crippled than a crippled fella who can't fecking act at all.' Except he said it ruder. *(Pause)* I thought I'd done alright for meself with me acting. Hours I practised in me hotel there. And all for nothing. *(Pause)* I gave it a go anyways. I had to give it a go. I had to get away from this place, Babbybobby, be any means, just like me mammy and daddy had to get away from this place. *(Pause)* Going drowning meself I'd often think of when I was here, just to . . . just to end the laughing at me, and the sniping at me, and the life of nothing but shuffling to the doctor's and shuffling back from the doctor's and pawing over the same oul books and finding any other way to piss another day away. Another day of sniggering, or the patting me on the head like a broken-brained gosawer. The village orphan. The village cripple, and nothing more. Well, there are plenty round here just as crippled as me, only it isn't on the outside it shows. *(Pause)* But the thing is, you're not one of them, Babbybobby, nor never were. You've a kind heart on you. I suppose that's why it was so easy to cod you with the TB letter, but that's why I was so sorry for codding you at the time and why I'm just as sorry now. Especially for codding you with the same thing your Mrs passed from. Just I thought that would be more effective. But in the long run, I thought, or I hoped, that if you had a choice between you being codded a while and me doing away with meself, once your anger had died down anyways, you'd choose you being codded every time. Was I wrong, Babbybobby? Was I?

Sloane – young

ENTERTAINING MR SLOANE JOE ORTON

This black comedy was first produced at Wyndham's Theatre, London, in 1964 and more recently at The Arts Theatre, London, in 2001.

Mr Sloane is a young psychopath, ruthless and single-minded. When he arrives at landlady Kath's house looking for a room, she and her brother, Ed, welcome him with open arms. He is such a nice young man and both are intent on seducing him. Only their elderly father, Kemp, is suspicious of **Sloane**, having seen him somewhere before. **Sloane** silences him by kicking him to death. Brother and sister now have **Sloane** exactly where they want him and each agree to 'share' him for six months of the year.

In this scene **Sloane** is alone with Kemp. He pulls the old man's stick away from him, pushes him into a chair and demands to know what he has been saying about him. Kemp foolishly accuses him of killing his 'old boss'.

From: *Orton, The Complete Plays – Master Playwrights*
Published by Methuen Drama

Sloane

Your vision is faulty. You couldn't identify nobody now. So long after. You said so yourself . . . Sit still! *(Silence)* . . . It was an accident, Pop. I'm innocent. You don't know the circumstances . . . Accidental death . . . You're pre-judging my case . . . Keep quiet. *(Silence)* It's like this see. One day I leave the Home. Stroll along. Sky blue. Fresh air. They'd found me a likeable permanent situation. Canteen facilities. Fortnight's paid holiday. Overtime? Time and a half after midnight. A staff dance each year. What more could one wish to devote one's life to? I certainly loved that place. The air round Twickenham was like wine. Then one day I take a trip to the old man's grave. Hic Jacets in profusion. Ashes to Ashes. Alas the fleeting. The sun was declining. A few press-ups on a tomb belonging to a family name of Cavaneagh, and I left the grave-yard. I thumbs a lift from a geyser who promises me a bed. Gives me a bath. And a meal. Very friendly. All you could wish he was, a photo-grapher. He shows me one or two experimental studies. An experience for the retina and no mistake. He wanted to photo me. For certain inter-esting features I had that he wanted the exclusive right of preserving. You know how it is. I didn't like to refuse. No harm in it I suppose. But then I got to thinking . . . I knew a kid once called MacBride that happened to. Oh, yes . . . so when I gets to think of this I decide I got to do something about it. And I gets up in the middle of the night looking for the film see. He has a lot of expensive equipment about in his studio see. Well it appears that he gets the wrong idea. Runs in. Gives a shout. And the long and the short of it is I loses my head which is a thing I never ought to a done with the worry of them photos an all. And I hits him. I hits him. *(Pause)* He must have had a weak heart. Something like that I should imagine. Definitely should have seen his doctor before that. I wasn't to know was I? I'm not to blame. *(Silence)*

Steve – aged 20

FLATMATES ELLEN DRYDEN

First workshopped and performed by the Chiswick Youth Theatre and published in 2000, the action takes place in a student flat in the 1990s.

Steve, a law student whose wealthy parents own the flat, lets out two rooms to Lynn and Tom, who are studying English.

In this opening scene, Steve is sitting at an old wooden dining table loaded with milk bottles, cartons and cornflake packets consuming a large breakfast. Lynn sits opposite him removing her nail varnish. They are both in a disagreeable mood. Tom joins them. He has been sitting up most of the night writing an essay and is not at his best. Steve has taken his milk and poured it into his coffee – they quarrel and Tom finally rushes out of the room. Steve comments that Tom is getting tiresome. Lynn starts to collect up her things. This is worse than sharing with her girlfriends Kate and Abbey: at least they only rowed about fellas. 'Wheels within undercurrents' are more than she can take.

From: *Six Primroses Each and other Plays for Young Actors*
Published by First Writes Publications, London

Steve

What a command of metaphor you do have, my dear Lynn. Strikes me all you English lot have got too much time on your hands and not enough intellectual meat . . .What was that you wrote – when you last wrote an essay that is – all that junk about the 'closely woven texture' of George Eliot's prose? Closely woven cerrap! It's unhealthy, all this poring over literature. Makes you think you've got feelings. You all need a dose of nice, detached, unemotional law . . . *(Pushing away his plate)* Now. What shall I have for lunch? There's a rather piquant little terrine of crab I've had my eye on for a while. But do I feel fishy today? And would Tom cast it in my face in a rage thinking I'd been at his tinned pilchards? . . . If he must work so hard to please that rancid little mouse of a mother of his, that's his problem . . . She believes Tom is the sun, the moon and the stars . . . A bloodsucker. Keeping poor old Tom scribbling little pictures labelled 'Mummy' and writing pathetic letters from 'your loving little son'. It's time he shoved her under a bus and went out and did something outrageous like going on the Tube without paying! Much better to have a mother like mine. She can just about remember who I am when I'm actually there. She lost interest in me when I stopped being a curly headed little accessory to her fashion photos . . . Tom's wound up so tight there'll be bits found all over the Home Counties when he finally splits! . . . Get out of the way! Don't be self-indulgent, Lynn. All you're really bothered about is a good time – so don't pretend to be all caring and compassionate about Tom. It's nauseating. Mummy'll come and pick up the pieces and put them in a plastic bag and take them home and stick them all together again. *(Pause)* I'm thinking of asking Tom to leave, actually . . . He's only paying me half of what you do, you know. Why should I subsidise Tom because I've had the forethought to have a rich Mummy and Daddy who look after me instead of a whinging little apology of a female who managed to get herself pregnant at fifteen and didn't do anything about it. I think it's unhealthy to have a mother who's only a few years older than you. And who was his Dad? Some visually handicapped passer-by? . . . never promise to keep secrets, Lynn dear. Much too exhausting.

Tom – American, young

THE GLASS MENAGERIE TENNESSEE WILLIAMS

First performed in London at the Theatre Royal, Haymarket, in 1948 and set in the Wingfield family apartment in a tenement building in St Louis, *The Glass Menagerie* is described as a 'memory' play.

Tom Wingfield recalls his life in St Louis with his mother, Amanda, and his crippled sister Laura. Amanda clings to the past and her memories of the 'gentlemen callers' who were once so numerous. Laura lives in a world of her own among her collection of glass animals. Meanwhile, **Tom** himself spends all his spare time in the cinema in order to escape the intolerable situation at home. When he arrives home with his friend Jim, Amanda welcomes the visitor as a potential 'gentleman caller' for her daughter. But although Jim is kind and sympathetic towards Laura he is already engaged to another girl. Amanda blames **Tom** for her daughter's disappoint-ment, accusing him of having known about his friend's engagement before bringing him home.

In this earlier scene, **Tom** is quarrelling with his mother. She has confiscated his books as she considers them unsuitable and tells him she is 'at the end of her patience'.

Published by Penguin Books, London

Tom

What do you think I'm at? Aren't I supposed to have any patience to reach the end of, Mother? I know, I know. It seems unimportant to you, what I'm *doing* – what I *want* to do – having a little *difference* between them! . . . Listen! You think I'm crazy about the *warehouse*? *(He bends fiercely toward her slight figure)* You think I'm in love with the Continental Shoemakers? You think I want to spend fifty-five *years* down there in that – *celotex interior*! with – *fluorescent* – *tubes*! Look! I'd rather somebody picked up a crowbar and battered out my brains – than go back mornings! I *go*! Every time you come in yelling that God damn *'Rise and Shine!' 'Rise and Shine!'* I say to myself, 'How *lucky dead* people are!' But I get up. *I go*! For sixty-five dollars a month I give up all that I dream of doing and being *ever*! And you say self – *self's* all I ever think of. Why, listen, if self is what I thought of, Mother, I'd be where he is – GONE! *(Pointing to father's picture)* As far as the system of transportation reaches! *(He starts past her. She grabs his arm)* Don't grab at me, Mother! . . . I'm going to the *movies*! . . . *(Crouching towards her, overtowering her tiny figure. She backs away, gasping)* I'm going to opium dens! Yes, opium dens, dens of vice and criminals' hang-outs, Mother. I've joined the Hogan gang, I'm a hired assassin, I carry a tommy-gun in a violin case! I run a string of cat-houses in the Valley! They call me Killer, Killer Wingfield, I'm leading a double-life, a simple, honest warehouse worker by day, by night a dynamic *tsar of the underworld, Mother*. I go to gambling casinos, I spin away fortunes on the roulette table! I wear a patch over one eye and a false moustache, sometimes I put on green whiskers. On those occasions they call me – *El Diablo*! Oh, I could tell you things to make you sleepless! My enemies plan to dynamite this place. They're going to blow us all sky-high some night! I'll be glad, very happy, and so will you! You'll go up, up on a broomstick, over Blue Mountain with seventeen gentlemen callers! You ugly – babbling old – *witch* . . . *(He goes)*.

Youngblood – early 20s, Black American

JITNEY AUGUST WILSON

First produced at the Royal National Theatre in 2001 and set in a jitney station in Pittsburg, Pennsylvania, where a firm of cab drivers serves the black neighbourhoods.

The station is run by Becker, a well-respected man in his 60s. His drivers are Turnbo, Fielding, Doub and **Youngblood**. **Youngblood** and his girlfriend, Rena, are struggling to make a life for themselves and their young son. **Youngblood** is hardly ever at home these days and rumour has it that he is running around with 'Peaches', Rena's sister.

In this scene Rena has called in at the station. **Youngblood** didn't come home last night and she accuses him of hiding things from her. He announces that he has put a deposit down on a house for her and wanted it to be a surprise. He has been working extra hours to pay for it. Rena is not pleased. He should have consulted her before he picked out a house for her. They should do things together: '. . . you did the right thing but you did it wrong.'

Published by Nick Hern Books, London

Youngblood

You want to know what I was hiding from you? I'll tell you. I been hustling . . . working day and night . . . while you accuse me of running the streets . . . and all I'm trying to do is save enough money so I can buy a house so you and Jesse have someplace decent to live. I asked Peaches if she would go with me to look at houses, cause I wanted to surprise you. I wanted to pull a truck up to the house and say, 'Come on, baby, we moving.' And drive on out to Penn Hills and pull that truck up in front of one of them houses and say, 'This is yours. This is your house baby.' That's what she was trying to hide from you. That's why Turnbo seen her riding in my car all the time. I found a house and I come up a hundred and fifty dollars short from closing the deal, and I come and took the eighty dollars out of the drawer . . . I wanted to surprise you . . . You always saying you don't want to live your whole life in the projects . . . Wait till you see it. It's real nice. It's all on one floor . . . it's got a basement . . . like a little den. We can put the TV down there. I told myself Rena's gonna like this. Wait till she see I bought her a house . . . No matter what I do it's gonna come out wrong with you. That's why you jump to conclusions. That's why you accused me of running around with Peaches. You can't look and see that I quit going to parties all the time . . . that I quit running with Ba Bra and Earl . . . that I quit chasing women. You just look at me and see the old Darnell. If you can't change the way you look at me . . . then I may as well surrender now. I can't beat your memory of who I was if you can't see I've changed. I go out here and work like a dog to try and do something nice for you and no matter what I do, I can't never do it right cause all you see is the way I used to be. You don't see the new Darnell. You don't see I've changed.

jitney a small bus carrying passengers for a low fare.

Raleigh – aged 18

JOURNEY'S END R C SHERRIFF

First produced at the Apollo Theatre in 1928 and set in March 1918 towards the end of the First World War.

The action takes place over three days in a dug-out in France and shows the effect of war on a group of young Officers – some of them not long out of school. **Second Lieutenant Raleigh** has been assigned to Captain Stanhope's Company. He is young and enthusiastic and welcomed by everyone with the exception of Stanhope, who is not at all happy about the new appointment.

In this early scene **Raleigh** has just arrived and introduces himself to Osborne, Stanhope's second in command. Osborne offers him a whiskey and asks if he knows Captain Stanhope.

Published by Penguin Books, London

Raleigh

Yes, rather! We were at school together – at least – of course – I was only a kid and he was one of the big fellows; he's three years older than I am . . . He was skipper of Rugger at Barford, and kept wicket for the eleven. A jolly good bat, too . . . Oh, I think he'll remember me. *(He stops, and goes on rather awkwardly)* You see, it wasn't only that we were just at school together; our fathers were friends, and Dennis used to come and stay with us in the holidays. Of course, at school I didn't see much of him, but in the holidays we were terrific pals . . . Last time he was on leave he came down to the school; he'd just got his MC and been made a captain. He looked splendid! It – sort of – made me feel . . . keen . . . Yes. Keen to get out here. I was frightfully keen to get into Dennis's regiment. I thought, perhaps, with a bit of luck I might get to the same battalion . . . I know. It's an amazing bit of luck. When I was at the base I did an awful thing. You see, my uncle's at the base – he has to detail officers to regiments – General Raleigh. I went to see him on the quiet and asked him if he could get me into this battalion. He bit my head off, and said I'd got to be treated like everybody else – and next day I was told I *was* coming to this battalion. Funny, wasn't it? . . . And when I got to Battalion Headquarters, and the colonel told me to report to 'C' Company, I could have cheered. I expect Dennis'll be frightfully surprised to see me. I've got a message for him. From my sister. You see, Dennis used to stay with us, and naturally my sister *(he hesitates)* – well – perhaps I ought not . . . They're not – er – officially engaged . . . She'll be awfully glad I'm with him here; I can write and tell her all about him. He doesn't say much in his letters; can we write often? *(There is a pause)* You don't think Dennis'll mind my – sort of – forcing myself into his company? I never thought of that; I was so keen.

Harry – Lancashire, aged 17

LOVE ON THE DOLE
RONALD GOW AND WALTER GREENWOOD

First performed at the Manchester Repertory Theatre in 1934 and in London at the Garrick Theatre in 1935, *Love on the Dole* is set in Hanky Park, Salford, Lancashire.

In Hanky Park in the 1930s, unemployment is high. Mr Hardcastle is on the dole and his wife takes in washing. Their daughter Sally works in a mill – the only one in the family bringing in a decent wage. Their son, **Harry**, earns 17 shillings a week in a machine shop at the local foundry, but already many of his fellow workers have been laid off. He is courting Helen, a 16-year-old local girl, and they are planning to get married. When he wins 22 pounds on the horses it seems like a fortune and he shares it among the family.

In this scene it is a year later and **Harry** has lost his job in the machine shop. Mrs Hardcastle is in the kitchen making up a bundle of things to take to the pawnshop when **Harry** comes in looking troubled. The Public Assistance Committee have cut his dole money and to make matters worse, Helen is pregnant.

Published by Samuel French, London

Harry

(Sits by the table and stares at the floor) Ma . . . I've got bad news . . . They've knocked me off the dole money . . . They've knocked me off the dole, I tell you . . . It's the Public Assistance Committee. They say the money's got to stop because Sally's working and Dad's getting the dole as it is. They say there's enough coming into one house . . . But – it's Helen I'm thinking of. You see, we were going to get married . . . I mean we've got to! . . . Ay – she's seen the doctor – we've got to . . . Look here, Ma, it isn't that I don't want to marry her. I do. I like her better than – well, anything, and we was planning to marry. We was going to make do on my dole money and what she's getting herself, and now this happens. If only we can get a start. I'll be drawing the dole again as soon as we are wed. And I thought perhaps – Well, I thought you and Dad would let her come here, and we could share the back room with Sally . . . Oh, gosh, Ma, it's driving me barmy. *(He breaks down and buries his face. Mrs Hardcastle turns to Harry and timidly puts her hand on his shoulder)* Sorry, Ma, but I'm ashamed to walk the streets. I feel they're all watching me. I've been to twenty places this morning and it's the same blasted story all the time. 'No hands wanted.' Though they don't usually say it so polite. And look at me clothes. It'll take six months' pay to buy new ones. Aw, God, just let me get a job. I don't care if it's only half-pay, but give me something . . . *(Hardcastle comes in from the street, hangs up his cap, looks from one to the other)* You see, Dad, I'll have to marry her and I thought . . . I thought, maybe, that we could come and live here and get a bed in back room with Sal . . . *(rises – warmly)* Hey! I'm not having you calling her a slut. Just you leave her name out of it . . . I'm asking you for nothing. I'm not the only one out of work in this house, remember. Yah, you treat me like a kid just because I've got nothing and I'm out of work. You didn't talk like that when I was sharing my winnings with you, did you? Once let me get hold of some money again and I'll never part with a penny of it. I'm supposed to be a man, I am – Well, look at me. Aye, and if there was another war you'd call me a man too. I'd be a bloody hero then . . . I don't want to live here. Do you understand? I wouldn't live with you if I got the chance. You can go to hell! I'm leaving here.

Puck

A MIDSUMMER NIGHT'S DREAM
WILLIAM SHAKESPEARE

A comedy written somewhere between 1595 and 1599, the action takes place in Athens as preparations are being made for the wedding of Duke Theseus and Hippolyta, Queen of the Amazons.

At the same time there is unrest in the Fairy Kingdom. The Fairy King, Oberon, has quarrelled with his Queen, Titania, over the possession of a little Indian boy whom she has taken under her protection. To punish her, Oberon sends his attendant sprite, **Puck**, to find a magic flower known as 'Love in Idleness'. Oberon squeezes the juice of this flower into Titania's eyes as she is sleeping in her secret bower, so that when she awakes she will fall in love with the first thing she sets eyes on.

In a wood nearby a group of Athenian workmen, lead by Bottom the weaver, are rehearsing a play – *Pyramus and Thisbe* – to be performed before the Duke on his wedding day. As Bottom finishes his scene and walks away from his fellow actors, **Puck** espies him and quickly places an ass's head on his shoulders.

In this scene **Puck** returns to tell Oberon his news. Titania has woken in her secret bower as Bottom entered through a brake in the hedge and has straightaway fallen in love with 'an ass'.

Published by Penguin Books, London

Puck

My mistress with a monster is in love.
Near to her close and consecrated bower,
While she was in her dull and sleeping hour,
A crew of patches, rude mechanicals
That work for bread upon Athenian stalls,
Were met together to rehearse a play
Intended for great Theseus' nuptial day.
The shallowest thickskin of that barren sort,
Who Pyramus presented, in their sport
Forsook his scene and entered in a brake,
When I did him at this advantage take.
An ass's nole I fixèd on his head.
Anon his Thisbe must be answerèd,
And forth my mimic comes. When they him spy –
As wild geese that the creeping fowler eye,
Or russet-pated choughs, many in sort,
Rising and cawing at the gun's report,
Sever themselves and madly sweep the sky –
So at his sight away his fellows fly,
And at our stamp here o'er and o'er one falls.
He 'Murder!' cries, and help from Athens calls.
Their sense thus weak, lost with their fears thus strong,
Made senseless things begin to do them wrong.
For briars and thorns at their apparel snatch,
Some sleeves, some hats. From yielders all things catch.
I led them on in this distracted fear,
And left sweet Pyramus translated there;
When in that moment – so it came to pass –
Titania waked, and straightway loved an ass.

Moses – young

MONSIEUR IBRAHIM AND THE FLOWERS OF THE QUR'AN

ERIC-EMMANUEL SCHMITT

TRANSLATED BY PATRICK DRIVER AND PATRICIA BENECKE

First produced at the Bush Theatre in 2006; set in Paris in 1960.

The two main characters are **Moses**, a 13-year-old Jewish boy, and Monsieur Ibrahim, a 70-year-old Muslim. (These two actors also play all the other parts mentioned in the script.)

Moses lives with a dour, unloving father who is forever criticising and comparing him unfavourably with his older brother, Popol – whom **Moses** has never seen. Every day after school he has to prepare and cook dinner for his father. He always buys tinned food from the local grocery and becomes friendly with the owner, Monsieur Ibrahim.

In this scene **Moses** returns home to find a note from his father saying he is leaving.

Published by Methuen Publishing, London

Moses

The following day, when I came back from school, I found a note on the floor of our dark hall. *(He looks at the paper. Recognises worriedly:)* That's my father's handwriting.

'Moses,
I am sorry, but I'm leaving. I simply don't have it in me to be a father.
Popo . . .'

That's crossed out. He probably wanted to say something about Popol like, 'With Popol, I could have made it, with you, I can't,' or, 'Popol would have given me the strength and energy to be a father, you don't,' or something of that ilk he didn't dare to write down in the end. Well, you didn't have to write it. I got the message, thanks very much.

'Maybe we'll meet again someday, when you're grown up. When I don't feel quite so ashamed and when you've found it in you to forgive me. Farewell.'

Farewell, exactly!

'P.S. What money I have left is on the table. Here is a list of people who need to know I'm gone. They'll take care of you.'

And then a list of four names I'd never heard.

I took a decision. I had to pretend.

No way would I admit to being abandoned, that was out of the question. Abandoned twice: once by my mother when I was born; a second time by my father when I was a teenager. If word got around, no one would give me the time of day. What was so repulsive about me? What did I have that made it impossible to love me?

My decision was irrevocable: I'd fake my father's presence. I'd make everyone think he still lived here, ate here, shared his long, tedious evenings with me . . . The money my father left me lasted a month. I learned to forge his signature to fill in the necessary forms, to answer letters from school. I kept cooking for both of us, served dinner for two each night; only that I threw his portion into the bin.

A few nights a week, for the benefit of the neighbours across the street, I sat in his chair with his pullover, his shoes, flour in my hair, and tried to read my beautiful, brand new Qur'an.

I had to prove to myself that I was lovable, I told myself that at school there was no time to lose: I had to fall in love. There wasn't much of a choice given that it was a boys' school; everyone was in love with the caretaker's daughter, Myriam. Although she was only thirteen, she had twigged she was ruling over three hundred panting pubescent boys. I started courting her with the ardour of a drowning man . . . Someone had to love me before the whole world discovered that even my parents, the only ones who had a duty to love me, had cleared off.

The Templar – aged about 20

NATHAN THE WISE
GOTTHOLD EPHRAIM LESSING
A VERSION BY EDWARD KEMP

This revival of a German classic was first performed at the Minerva Theatre, Chichester in 2003 and transferred to the Hampstead Theatre, London in 2005. Set in Jerusalem in 1193, it is a plea for religious tolerance.

Nathan, a rich Jew, learns that a Knight Templar has rescued his daughter Rachel from a terrible fire. He is anxious to meet him, but the **Templar** wants nothing to do with a Jew. Nathan persists and eventually they shake hands and he arranges for the young man to meet Rachel.

The **Templar** confesses to Daya, a Christian woman who has brought Rachel up from a child, that he 'loves Rachel to distraction'. But how can a Christian marry a Jew? Daya lets him into a secret: Rachel is not a Jew. She was born to Christian parents, but Nathan raised her as his own daughter in the Jewish faith.

The **Templar** seeks advice from his Confessor, who tells him that to bring up a Christian child in the Jewish faith is sin punishable only by death.

In this scene the Sultan has summoned the **Templar** to his palace. He asks him why he is suspicious of Nathan . . .

Published by Nick Hern Books, London

Templar

I've nothing against Nathan. Nathan is Nathan. I'm angry with myself
. . . For dreaming that a Jew could cease to be Jew. For dreaming it with
my eyes wide open . . . Nathan's daughter. I did for her what I did
because I did it. But I didn't want her thanks, I didn't want anything
from them, so I refused to see her, despite many requests. Nathan comes
home, he learns what's happened, he seeks me out, he thanks me, we

he hopes that I might grow to like his daughter. So having been
persuaded I come to the house, and there I find a girl, a girl of

I am ashamed of myself . . . If Nathan hadn't encouraged me, then
maybe I could have resisted but I am a fool. I leapt into the flames again.
And this time I was rejected . . . By Nathan. Oh, he doesn't dismiss me
outright. No, he's too shrewd for that. He has to make enquiries, think
things over, needs time. Well, we could all do that. Why didn't I take
some time to consider the situation while the flames were licking at her
ankles? That would have been wise . . . You think he has no prejudices
just because he appears so rational, so open-minded? I don't believe we
ever lose the superstitions of our race. We drink them in with our
mother's milk, and we may mock them but they are bred into our bones
. . . and sometimes they are so ingrained we don't even know they're
there, and sometimes we indulge them because they are our own . . . I
thought so too. And what if you heard this paragon was actually so
fervent in his faith that he sought to obtain Christian children and raise
them up as Jews? . . . The girl, the same girl he lured me with, the girl
he says is his daughter, is no such thing. She's a Christian child taken
from God knows where . . . He's unmasked. The prophet of tolerance
is shown for what he is. A Jewish wolf . . . Why should I be calm? Why
should Jews and Muslims have their rights and Christians be denied?

'Mark – aged 17

NEW BOY FROM A NOVEL BY WILLIAM SUTCLIFFE
ADAPTED BY RUSSELL LABEY

First performed at the Pleasance Theatre, Edinburgh in 2000 and at the Pleasance Theatre, London in 2001.

When a new boy, Barry, joins the Sixth Form at a North London School, **Mark** decides to take him under his wing – with disastrous results.

In this early scene, set in the changing room after rugby, Barry asks **Mark** to tell him about Parents' Evenings. What are they like?

Published by Amber Lane Press, Oxford

Mark

Parents' evenings . . . An orgy of social embarrassment – I love them. It's also a good opportunity to see who has the fittest mother. Jeremy Dorlin's is quite nice, so is Robert Konisberg's, which for an ugly boy comes as a pleasant surprise – best post-forty arse in the whole of Edgware. All the Christians have ugly mothers, oh, except for yours, I'm sure, and Peter Pillow's, the vicar's son, whose mother has the subtle allure of a shaggable nun. The Asian mums are occasionally horny with the odd fit daughter in tow. All the Edgware Jewish mothers are dressed in high heels, stone-washed jeans and fur jackets with shoulder-length hair curled and dyed red. They wear so much make-up they have to pout all evening to stop it falling off in chunks. Stanmore Jewish mothers go for the drab but overdressed combo, leaving only the Hampstead and Golders Green set to dress with any style . . . The fathers fall into two groups: brown and white. Other than that they're indistinguishable. The Christian fathers are easier to tell apart, tending to divide neatly into two categories: Volvo drivers: classy – and BMW drivers: yobs made good . . . My parents hardly listen to the teachers and spend most of the interviews nervously flicking through my form list trying to figure out who they're going to bump into in the corridor next. Besides, my school-work's always good. My dad has only ever said one thing to me after a parents' evening . . . 'Never become a teacher.'

Romeo – young

ROMEO AND JULIET WILLIAM SHAKESPEARE

A tragedy written in or around 1595, and set in Verona, it is the story of two 'star-crossed lovers', **Romeo Montague** and Juliet Capulet, whose tragic deaths end their families' long-standing feud.

Romeo and Juliet meet and fall in love at a feast given by Juliet's father. The hatred between the Montagues and the Capulets makes it impossible for them to be together and so **Romeo** persuades Friar Lawrence to marry them secretly. After the ceremony **Romeo** is confronted by Juliet's cousin, Tybalt, who challenges him to a duel. **Romeo** refuses to fight, but his friend, Mercutio, takes up the challenge and is killed under **Romeo**'s arm as he tries to separate them. In fury **Romeo** fights and kills Tybalt, then, persuaded by his companions, runs from the scene.

Romeo is hiding out in the Friar's cell, when the Friar arrives bringing good news. The Duke has not imposed the expected death sentence, but instead has sentenced **Romeo** to banishment. He must leave Verona and Juliet.

Published by Penguin Books, London

Romeo

'Tis torture, and not mercy. Heaven is here,
Where Juliet lives. And every cat and dog
And little mouse, every unworthy thing,
Live here in heaven and may look on her.
But Romeo may not. More validity,
More honourable state, more courtship lives
In carrion flies than Romeo. They may seize
On the white wonder of dear Juliet's hand
And steal immortal blessing from her lips,
Who, even in pure and vestal modesty,
Still blush, as thinking their own kisses sin.
This may flies do, when I from this must fly.
And sayest thou yet that exile is not death?
But Romeo may not, he is banishèd.
Flies may do this but I from this must fly.
They are free men. But I am banishèd.
Hadst thou no poison mixed, no sharp-ground knife,
No sudden mean of death, though ne'er so mean,
But 'banishèd' to kill me – 'banishèd'?
O' Friar, the damnèd use that word in hell.
Howling attends it! How hast thou the heart,
Being a divine, a ghostly confessor,
A sin-absolver, and my friend professed,
To mangle me with that word 'banishèd'?

Lee – aged 15

SCHOOL PLAY SUZY ALMOND

First produced at the Soho Theatre, London, in 2001.

Charlie Silver is bad news in her South London comprehensive school: a problem to teachers and a bad influence on the rest of the class. Her ambitions are to front a gang, ride a motorbike and to 'mess with teachers' heads'. She boasts a long list of teachers who have given up on her account. Then Miss Fry, the new music teacher, arrives and things begin to change. Charlie is given countless detentions, but unknown to her 'gang' – **Lee Coulson** who has recently been suspended from school, and his friend Paul – is using these detention periods to develop her suppressed musical talents.

In this scene, Charlie is at the piano waiting for Miss Fry to arrive when **Lee** comes bursting in. He accuses her of letting him down. She was supposed to meet him and Paul in the car park earlier that afternoon with her customised Hollister bike on which he was to ride 'a lap of honour' against his rival, Danny Chapel. Charlie says she has a music exam the next day and needed to practise. She tries to explain to him what playing the piano means to her and how Miss Fry has changed her way of thinking – not only about the music, but also about herself. **Lee** pulls out a piece of paper from his pocket. It is an internal report with confidential information about the students. He reads out the report that Miss Fry has written about Charlie.

Published by Oberon Books, London

Lee

Charlie . . . *(Pulling out a piece of paper from his pocket)* Look at this . . . I used to have a white bike and I applied excellence in keeping it clean. I fought for it, I was up against the weather. Some of these teachers, they don't apply so much excellence in their day to day business, they leave things lying around. Confidential information about students. Just cos you don't have to be the best – don't mean you're allowed to be the worst . . . And another internal report. It was left on the desk in the Physics room with a load of others. Paul's sister got hold of it a few days ago . . . I won't read both pages, just the Miss Fry one . . . Profile. Charlie Silver. Charlie is fifteen years old. Charlie's er . . . Charlie's brother was killed in a motorbike accident twelve months ago . . . Charlie's behaviour in class is consistently aggressive. She finds it difficult to socialise with other children, particularly girls. She cannot concentrate and an incident with a fire extinguisher last year confirmed that she is . . . confirmed that she is a disruptive force, to the detriment of the other children's progress . . . *(Turning to next page)* Blah blah blah . . . Music Report from Miss Fry . . . I am worried about how Charlie will react to my leaving. She has become very attached to me and I think she will find it very hard to settle into working with a new teacher. She is impatient with her practice and can be clumsy – but when her wilfulness translates into enthusiasm she tries very hard and she has recently warmed as a personality, even giving me chocolates after lessons as a thank you. *(Charlie snatches it from him)* Are you okay? . . . I tried to tell you. I'm sorry. I mean it . . . I shouldn't have brought it. But she shouldn't have left it lying around. It's not just you, there's a load flying around school, they were found a few days ago, got photocopied. Charlie, she was taking you for a ride. She's a half-arsed supply teacher, making out she was a permanent. That's what they all do – they think we're stupid . . . *(Pause)* I could of told you at the start that you don't learn music from a teacher. It comes from the street: Learning what joins one beat to the next. Running lyrical rings around people who think that reading and writing makes them the big I am. Classroom knocks the stuffing out of you.

Tony Lumpkin – aged 17–20

SHE STOOPS TO CONQUER OLIVER GOLDSMITH

This 18th century comedy was first produced at the Theatre Royal, Covent Garden, London, in 1773. It is set in the Hardcastles' country mansion and parodies the sentimental comedies popular at that time.

The action revolves around the arranged match and courtship between the Hardcastles' daughter Kate and Young Marlow, and the practical jokes played on family and friends by **Tony Lumpkin**, Mrs Hardcastle's son by a former marriage. **Tony** has been ordered by his mother to marry his cousin, Constance, but he wants nothing to do with her. When he discovers she is in love with Marlow's friend, Hastings, he is only too delighted to help the lovers elope together. His mother discovers the plot and insists on accompanying Constance to her Aunt Pedigree's home, 30 miles away. **Tony** takes charge of the coach journey, driving them round and round the neighbouring countryside, finally tipping everyone into the local duck pond. Here he describes the adventure to Hastings, whose only concern is for Constance's safety.

Published by New Mermaids

Tony

Ay, I'm your friend, and the best friend you have in the world, if you knew but all. This riding by night, by the bye, is cursedly tiresome. It has shook me worse than the basket of a stage-coach . . . Five and twenty miles in two hours and a half is no such bad driving. The poor beasts have smoked for it: rabbit me, but I'd rather ride forty miles after a fox, than ten with such varment . . . Left them? Why where should I leave them, but where I found them? . . . Riddle me this then. What's that goes round the house, and round the house, and never touches the house? . . . Why, that's it, mon. I have led them astray. By jingo, there's not a pond or slough within five miles of the place but they can tell the taste of . . . You shall hear. I first took them down Feather-bed Lane, where we stuck fast in the mud. I then rattled them crack over the stones of Up-and-down Hill – I then introduced them to the gibbet on Heavy-tree Heath, and from that, with a circumbendibus, I fairly lodged them in the horsepond at the bottom of the garden . . . No, no. Only mother is confoundedly frightened. She thinks herself forty miles off. She's sick of the journey, and the cattle can scarce crawl. So if your own horses be ready, you may whip off with cousin, and I'll be bound that no soul here can budge a foot to follow you . . . Ay, now it's dear friend, noble Squire. Just now, it was all idiot, cub, and run me through the guts. Damn your way of fighting, I say. After we take a knock in this part of the country, we kiss and be friends. But if you had run me through the guts, then I should be dead, and you might go kiss the hangman . . . Never fear me. Here she comes. Vanish. She's got from the pond, and draggled up to the waist like a mermaid . . . *(Enter* Mrs Hardcastle*)* Alack, mama, it was all your own fault. You would be for running away by night, without knowing one inch of the way.

smoked	galloped at speed
rabbit me	like 'drat me', a meaningless oath
varment	vermin; hence, objectionable people (first usage). He is talking about his mother and cousin
circumbendibus	roundabout process
cattle	stable slang for 'horses'
draggled	dirtied by being dragged through wet mud
quickset	hedge a hedge formed of 'quick' – i.e. living – plants

Oggy Moxon – aged 16–17

TEECHERS JOHN GODBER

First performed by the Hull Truck Company at the Edinburgh Festival in 1987 and set in a School Hall with a wooden stage, desks and chairs.

School leavers, Salty, Hobby and Gail, are presenting a play about life at Whitewall High – described as a comprehensive school somewhere in England, with its fair share of problems. All three play different characters, sometimes acting as narrators. In this scene Gail plays 'Bobby Moxon' – the cock of Whitewall High – known to all and sundry as 'Oggy Moxon'. ('Oggy' can be played either as 'Oggy' himself or as Gail playing 'Oggy'.)

From: John Godber: *Five Plays*
Published by Penguin Books, London

Note: If a male actor is playing 'Oggy' then you need to cut the lines from 'I knew that he fancied me' to 'somebody ought to drop him' and then take it up again from the line 'Oggy Moxon's speech about being hard' and continue to the end of the extract.

Oggy Moxon

The cock of Whitewall High was Bobby Moxon, known to all and sundry as – Oggy Moxon. There was no doubt at all that Oggy was dangerous, all the teachers gave him a wide berth. He was sixteen going on twenty-five. Rumour had it that he had lost his virginity when he was ten and that Miss Prime fancied the pants off him . . . One Wednesday, I was stood outside one of the mobile classrooms. Mr Dean had sent me out of class. I'd told him that I thought Peter the Great was a bossy gett! And he sent me out. I'm stood there with a mood on when Oggy comes past . . . I knew that he fancied me. *(As Oggy)* What you doing? *(As Gail)* Waiting for Christmas, what's it look like? *(As Oggy)* I'm having a party in my dad's pub, wanna come? Most of the third year is coming. Should be a good night . . . Might see you there . . . Wear something that's easy to get off. Your luck might be in. *(As Gail)* I hate him . . . Somebody ought to drop him . . . Oggy Moxon's speech about being hard: I'm Oggy Moxon . . . We said you'd have to use your imaginations. I'm Oggy, I'm as hard as nails, as toe-capped boots I'm hard, as marble in church, as concrete on your head I'm hard. As calculus I'm hard. As learning Hebrew is hard, then so am I. Even Basford knows I'm rock, his cane wilts like an old sock. And if any teachers in the shitpot school with their degrees and bad breath lay a finger on me, God be my judge, I'll have their hides. And if not me, our Nobby will be up to this knowledge college in a flash. All the female flesh fancy me in my five-o-ones, no uniform for me never. From big Mrs Grimes to pert Miss Prime I see their eyes flick to my button-holed flies. And they know like I that no male on this staff could satisfy them like me, cos I'm hard all the time. Last Christmas dance me and Miss Prime pranced to some bullshit track and my hand slipped down her back, and she told me she thought that I was great, I felt that arse, that schoolboy wank, a tight-buttocked, Reebok-footed, leggy-arse . . . I touched that and heard her sigh . . . for me. And as I walk my last two terms through these corridors of sickly books and boredom, I see grown men flinch and fear. In cookery one day my hands were all covered with sticky paste, and in haste I asked pretty Miss Bell if she could get for me an hanky from my pockets, of course she would, a student on teaching practice – wanting to help, not knowing my pockets had holes and my underpants were in the wash. 'Oh, no,' she yelped, but in truth got herself a thrill, and has talked of nothing else these last two years. Be warned, when Oggy Moxon is around get out your cigs . . . And lock up your daughters . . .

Dog

THE WITCH OF EDMONTON THOMAS DEKKER, JOHN FORD & WILLIAM ROWLEY

A tragicomedy written in 1621 and often performed at The Cockpit in Drury Lane. One of its more recent productions was by the Royal Shakespeare Company at the Other Place in Stratford in 1981.

Old Mother Sawyer – the Witch – has sold her soul to the devil, who appeared to her in the shape of a black **Dog**, so that she might be revenged on all those who harmed her. At the same time **Dog** has befriended Cuddy, a simple village boy, who has no idea that his friend 'Tommy' is in reality the devil in one of his many disguises. Now 'Tommy' has gone missing for several days. The Witch's powers have begun to wane and she is captured and condemned to hang.

In this scene **Dog** appears to Cuddy for the last time as a white dog. Cuddy recognises him by his bark and stops to speak to him. **Dog** boasts of his devilish exploits. He explains to Cuddy how he lured him into Edmonton marsh when they first met, by changing into the shape of Kate Carter, the village girl Cuddy was chasing after.

Published by New Mermaids

Dog

Hast thou forgot me? . . . *(Barks)* I have deluded thee
For sport to laugh at. The wench thou seekst
After thou never spakst with, but a spirit
In her form, habit and likeness. Ha, ha! . . .
I'll thus much tell thee. Thou never art so distant
From an evil spirit, but that thy oaths,
Curses and blasphemies pull him to thine elbow.
Thou never tellst a lie, but that a Devil
Is within hearing it; thy evil purposes
Are ever haunted; but when they come to act,
As thy tongue slandering, bearing false witness,
Thy hand stabbing, stealing, cosening, cheating,
He's then within thee. Thou playst, he bets upon thy part;
Although thou lose, yet he will gain by thee . . .
The old cadaver of some self-strangled wretch
We sometimes borrow, and appear human.
The carcass of some disease-slain strumpet,
We varnish fresh, and wear as her first beauty.
Didst never hear? if not, it has been done.
An hot luxurious lecher in his twines,
When he has thought to clip his dalliance,
There has provided been for his embrace
A fine hot flaming Devil in her place . . .
Why? These are all my delights, my pleasures, fool . . .
Ha, ha! The worse thou heardst of me, the better 'tis.
Shall I serve thee, fool, at the self-same rate? . . .
I am for greatness now . . .
Hence silly fool,
I scorn to prey on such an atom soul.

Thou . . . thee	Since the Devil's agent is giving conventional Puritan doctrine here, the speech is both polemical and satirical
twines	embraces
When . . . dalliance	when the Devil embraces the lecher
ducking . . . delight	The use of water spaniels for duck hunting was a popular sport
atom	tiny, irrelevant

audition speeches
for women

Agnes – young

AGNES OF GOD JOHN PIELMEIER

First presented in a staged reading at the Eugene O'Neill Playwrights Conference in 1979 at the Actors Theatre of Louisville in 1980. It opened on Broadway at the Music Box Theatre in 1982.

Doctor Martha Livingstone has been appointed by the Court to assess **Agnes**, a young nun accused of killing her new-born baby. **Agnes** is a simple girl who has spent most of her life in the convent with little or no contact with the outside world. She denies all knowledge of a baby. The Mother Superior objects strongly to her being questioned and applies to have the Doctor taken off the case, but eventually **Agnes** agrees to submit to hypnosis in order to build up a picture of what happened to her.

In this earlier scene, Doctor Livingstone asks **Agnes** how babies are born.

Published by Samuel French, US

Agnes

I don't know what you're talking about! You want to talk about the baby, everybody wants to talk about the baby, but I never saw the baby, so I can't talk about the baby, because I don't believe in the baby! . . . No! I'm tired of talking! I've been talking for weeks! And nobody believes me when I tell them anything! Nobody listens to *me*! . . . Where do *you* think babies come from? . . . Well, I think they come from when an angel lights on their mother's chest and whispers into her ear. That makes good babies start to grow. Bad babies come from when a fallen angel squeezes in down there, and they grow and grow until they come out down there. I don't know where good babies come out. *(Silence)* And you can't tell the difference except that bad babies cry a lot and make their fathers go away and their mothers get very ill and die sometimes. Mummy wasn't very happy when *she* died and I think she went to hell because every time I see her she looks like she just stepped out of a hot shower. And I'm never sure if it's her or the Lady who tells me things. They fight over me all the time. The Lady I saw when I was ten. I was lying on the grass looking at the sun and the sun became a cloud and the cloud became the Lady, and she told me she would talk to me and then her feet began to bleed and I saw there were holes in her hands and in her side and I tried to catch the blood as it fell from the sky but I couldn't see any more because my eyes hurt because there were big black spots in front of them. And she tells me things like – right now she's crying 'Marie! Marie!' but I don't know what that means. And she uses me to sing. It's as if she's throwing a big hook through the air and it catches me under my ribs and tries to pull me up but I can't move because Mummy is holding my feet and all I can do is sing in her voice, it's the Lady's voice, God loves you! *(Silence)* God loves you. *(Silence)* . . . I don't want to talk anymore, all right? I just want to go home.

Lulu – early 20s; Manchester

ALL THE ORDINARY ANGELS NICK LEATHER

First performed at the Royal Exchange, Manchester in 2005. The action takes place in and around Raffa's ice-cream factory in Manchester in 1989.

Ice-cream man Guiseppe Raffa has decided to retire and sets his two sons, Rocco and Lino, in competition with each other. The winner will get the family business; the loser will be left with nothing. The fight for customers soon becomes a deadly struggle between the two brothers.

Lulu works in the factory and has invented her own special ice-cream. She invites Rocco to try some, and it tastes so good that he decides to sell it under the name of 'Angelato'. Soon all the children of Manchester are demanding 'Angelato'. No one can compete with it, not even Lino. But now children are beginning to fall sick and no one can find out why.

This scene takes place in 'The Hidden Gem' – a local Roman Catholic church. Guiseppe is kneeling at the altar as **Lulu** enters. She kneels beside him. He has decided to sell the business and tells her he will soon become a rich man. As he gets up to go, **Lulu** stops him.

Published by Methuen, London

Lulu

The children of Manchester are sick, Giuseppe Raffa, and it's all your fault . . . there's a little kid, in the Royal, on a life-support machine . . . He overdosed. His parents don't know how. The police don't know how . . . There's coke in the ice cream, y'know . . . We've been puttin' cocaine in the mix. That's what Angelato is . . . I made it first. But it was never meant to be for sale – was just for me. *(Beat.)* Then Rocco tasted it. *(Beat.)* He wanted to win so bad. And it tasted so good. Seemed funny at first – and when it started to sell . . . *(Beat.)* but now I've not got nothin' – and no one – and that kid's in hospital – and it doesn't seem funny any more . . . A little bit makes such a lot o' difference. Makes the ice cream taste *so* . . . ice-creamy . . . People can't get enough o' the stuff. They want it without hardly knowin' why. Eat it, and they're the life and soul. But half an hour later when things are back to normal, it's more ice cream they want. And only Angelato'll do . . . We did it for you. Did it to win. There might've been a time when ice cream on its own was enough – when ice cream was everything – but that's gone. *(Beat.)* People wanted more. So we gave 'em more . . . Rocco can't stop. He's out o' control. *(Beat.)* I'm gonna go to the police. I've got to . . . They need to know.

Joni – 16

ANCIENT LIGHTS SHELAGH STEPHENSON

First performed at the Hampstead Theatre Club in November 2000 and set in a country cottage in Northumberland at Christmas, where Bea has invited her oldest friends – Kitty, Tom Cavallero and Tom's girlfriend, Iona – to spend the holiday with her and her new lover, Tad.

Tom is a Hollywood actor and Iona is making a documentary film about his life. Bea's daughter, **Joni**, is also staying over Christmas but would much rather be with her friends in Shepherd's Bush. Nevertheless, she is anxious to be part of the filming.

In this scene it is two o'clock in the morning and **Joni** is playing out an imaginary scene in which she is being interviewed about her 'first film role'. She is posing by a chair in her nightdress, trying to look provocative. She is interrupted by Tom before she has completed her 'interview' and dashes out of the room, mortified.

Published by Methuen Drama

Joni

(Lights up, later. Two a.m. Spotlight on Joni posing by the chair in her nightdress. Wild applause, wolf-whistles, camera bulbs flashing. Screen images washing over the set. She strikes a series of provocative poses as the applause dies down)

Yeah, I'm really really happy that the truth's out at last. Yeah, he gave me this ring. *(She holds out her hand)* It belonged to his mother, so you know, it seemed right. Right, it's incredible, I know, my first film and I'm nominated for an Oscar, I can't believe it, it's been an amazing year. Well, I've known Tom since I was tiny, so I've never been in awe of him or anything, and getting the film was nothing to do with our relationship because I'd already got the part before all this happened. Yeah, I met Iona a couple of times, and it was really terrible about the car crash and everything, but I think the relationship was more or less over by then. Decapitated. She never knew what hit her. I think I probably helped him to get over it. Well, it takes a bit of getting used to being over here in Beverly Hills with all the palm trees and everything, it's not much like Hammersmith, I can tell you. And getting mobbed by fans and not being able to leave the house. I've had a couple of stalkers, you know, the usual, God it's so boring. I can't go places like the supermarket any more, but we have staff and everything. Would I take my clothes off on film? I think that's a very difficult question, but yes, if the part demanded it –

(Lights change abruptly as Tom comes in, still in his bathrobe, clutching his mobile phone and a glass of whisky. He's sniffing, as if he's taken coke, and is obviously mid-conversation)

Tom . . . I was just going to bed, goodnight – *(She dashes out, mortified)*.

Charlotte – American, 15

A BRIEF HISTORY OF HELEN OF TROY OR EVERYTHING WILL BE DIFFERENT
MARK SCHULTZ

Originally produced in the US by the Soho Repertory Theatre and first performed in the UK at the Drum Theatre, Plymouth.

Charlotte is grief-stricken by the death of her beautiful mother, and her relationship with her father is becoming increasingly difficult. She is obsessed by Helen of Troy and her fantasies of becoming an object of desire start to spill over into normal life.

In this scene she is talking to her Guidance Counsellor, who refuses to help her become a 'porn star'.

Published by Oberon Modern Plays, London

Charlotte

So like, seeing as I'm made for sex? I'm gonna be in porn . . . It's what I want. I've read about it. I've done a lot of research. Porn is like a very nicely paying industry. And it is an industry. It's not like some flash in the pan sort of thing like some Internet thing or I don't know. It's been around. A while. There are videos and magazines. And if you're a woman? People love you. And they want to have sex with you. And they fantasise about you? And that's what I want . . . I think porn and I are a great match . . . Realistic? Okay? What does that mean anyway? I don't think you know what is realistic. I don't think you know what I can do. What I'm capable of. Do you give this advice to everyone? You're being unrealistic? What if I said, I want to be a doctor. What if I said, A doctor. Or what if maybe I said I want to be the president. Like your president. And you'd vote for me and everything. What if I said that? Would that be realistic? More realistic? 'Cause I don't even know what that means. So tell me . . . You're supposed to be supportive. Right? You're supposed to support me. And help me. So help me be a porn star . . . Guide me . . . When I'm famous? You will be so sorry . . . You will think to yourself, God, I should have helped her and everything. I should have just helped her realise that dream. That goal. I could have become like, her inspiration. Like the wind beneath her wings or whatever. I hate that song. But it's over now. Now you're gonna like in the future when I'm famous you're gonna be sad. I will be so beautiful. Like my mom. You seen my mom? No. 'Cause she wouldn't even look at you. And now she's dead and don't even try to comfort me.

I'm gonna be beautiful. And you're gonna want me . . . No. Okay? No. It's over. It's over. You're gone. Okay? You're through. You and me are over . . . You hurt me. Okay? You hurt me. You're supposed to help me and, you hurt me. But okay whatever. Whatever doesn't kill me makes me I don't know something. But it's a good something. I have dreams. Needs. I am a star. Okay?

Grusha – young

THE CAUCASIAN CHALK CIRCLE
BERTOLT BRECHT
TRANSLATED FROM THE GERMAN BY JAMES AND TANIA STERN
WITH W H AUDEN

First performed at the Berliner Ensemble in 1954, this translation was published in 1960.

When the Governor's palace in Grusinia is stormed and the Governor taken away and executed, his baby son Michael is abandoned by his mother and his nurse. **Grusha**, a young kitchen maid, takes pity on the child and flees with him into the Northern Mountains. After many adventures, she is brought before the drunken rogue, Judge Asdak. The Governor's widow has demanded that Michael be returned to her and asks the court to restore custody. The Judge is on the widow's side and threatens to fine **Grusha** 20 piastres for contempt of court.

In this scene **Grusha** accuses the Judge of bribe-taking and corruption.

Published by Methuen, London – Methuen Student Edition

Grusha

That's a fine kind of Justice. You jump on us because we don't talk so refined as that lot with their lawyers . . . You want to pass the child on to her. She who is too refined even to know how to change its nappies! You don't know any more about Justice than I do, that's clear . . . I'll tell you what I think of your justice, you drunken onion! How dare you talk to me as though you were the cracked Isaiah on the church window! When they pulled you out of your mother, it wasn't planned that you'd rap her over the knuckles for pinching a little bowl of corn from somewhere! Aren't you ashamed of yourself when you see how afraid I am of you? But you've let yourself become their servant. So that their houses are not taken away, because they've stolen them. Since when do houses belong to bed-bugs? But you're on the look-out, otherwise they couldn't drag our men into their wars. You bribe-taker!

Azdak gets up. He begins to beam. With a little hammer he knocks on the table half-heartedly as if to get silence. But as Grusha's scolding continues, he only beats time with it

I've no respect for you. No more than for a thief or a murderer with a knife, who does what he wants. You can take the child away from me, a hundred against one, but I tell you one thing: for a profession like yours, they ought to choose only bloodsuckers and men who rape children. As a punishment. To make them sit in judgment over their fellow men, which is worse than swinging from the gallows.

Nicola – Leicester, teenage

CITY SUGAR STEPHEN POLIAKOFF

First presented at the Bush Theatre, London, in 1975 and then at the Comedy Theatre, London, in the following year.

The action takes place in the Sound Studio of a commercial radio station in Leicester, where disc-jockey Leonard Brazil is running a competition for his teenaged listeners. The coveted prize is to meet one of the boys from the pop group, The Yellow Jacks, at their concert in Leicester, and then to travel to London with them and stay there for four days at the expense of the studio. One of the 'phone-in' contestants is **Nicola Davies**, who works at the local supermarket.

In this scene **Nicola** has been brought into the studio. She has fought her way through the preliminary stages of the contest and has reached the final. So far she has answered most of the questions correctly and is neck-to-neck with the other finalist, Jane. She is seated in front of the microphone and Leonard asks her to talk for one minute on 'the last pop concert she went to'.

Published by Samuel French, London

Nicola

The last – the last pop concert I went to . . . it was here in Leicester – *(she swallows)* – and Ross and the group were playing, and I queued to get in for a long time . . . I don't know, not . . . We queued for a day and a night, I think – it was a bit wet – you see, and the stone, the pavement, was very hard and cold, much harder than you think – because we slept there you see – it was all right and – and then a man came up, it was late you know then, dark and everything, and he'd come to sell us hot dogs and things, he came out there and he set up along the side of the queue, it was a very long queue, and then soon another – another came up out of the dark, and then there was another one, till there were lots and lots all along the line, really close. *(She looks up)* . . . Oh! I thought it was enough . . . Oh – and – *(lost for words, she is extremely nervous)* – and then we went inside – and the concert – and it was them of course, and it was, you know – well it was all squashed – and some people rushed up and fought to get close – and there was a bit of biting, and that sort of thing, when they called out to us; they seemed a long way off – a very long way away, in their yellow and everything. They weren't very loud but they made you feel – I felt something come up, you know, a little sort of . . . *(A second of slightly clenched feeling)* I got, you know, a bit worked up inside – they were moving very slowly on the stage like they'd been slowed down, made me feel strange – then they held things up, waved it at us, smiling and everything, they waved yellow scarves, Ross had a bit of yellow string he waved. I think it was, a bit of yellow rope, and I half wanted to kick the girl in front of me or something because I couldn't see; all the way through I had to look at her great back, pressed right up against it. I remember I half wanted to get at it. Move it. And I nearly dropped a ring. *(Pulling at her finger)* I'd been pulling at, put it on specially. *(Very nervously)* If you drop anything it's gone for ever, you know – can't bend down if you're standing – and if you drop yourself – then you'd be gone. When you rush out at the end, you can see all the millions of things that have been dropped shining all over the floor, nobody gets a chance to pick them up. And then it was finished – you know, the concert, and I came outside. It was cold, I was feeling a bit funny. Just walked along out there and I thought maybe I was bleeding. I looked but I wasn't. Some people like to be after a concert, but I wasn't.

Margaret Knox – 18

FANNY'S FIRST PLAY GEORGE BERNARD SHAW

First performed at the Little Theatre in the Adelphi in 1911. It is a play within a play.

Fanny, a sheltered young girl brought up in Italy, has been sent to Cambridge to complete her education. Now she has written a play and for her birthday asks her father to arrange a private showing to an invited audience including four drama critics, but concealing the fact that she is the author. The play questions middle-class morality, suggesting that 'the young had better have their souls awakened by disgrace, capture by the police, and a month's hard labour, than drift from their cradles to their graves doing what other people do for no other reason than that other people do it, and know nothing of good and evil'. Her father is shocked. By the end of the performance, one of the critics has guessed quite correctly that the heroine, '**Margaret**', is in fact based on Fanny herself.

In the play **Margaret Knox**, the daughter of a respectable shop-keeper and his deeply religious wife, fails to return home after attending a prayer meeting with her Aunt. A fortnight later she walks in accompanied by a young French marine officer. She announces that she has been in Holloway Gaol where she was sent for assaulting a policeman and knocking out two of his teeth. Her parents are upset – she has brought disgrace on the family.

In this scene she is alone with her mother, who is trying to reason with her. **Margaret** makes light of the incident: she had enjoyed the experience. Mrs Knox says she hates to see her daughter so hardened.

This edition published in 1921 by Constable and Company Ltd, London
Re-issued by Penguin in 1987

Margaret

I'm not hardened, mother. But I can't talk nonsense about it. You see, it's all real to me. I've suffered it. I've been shoved and bullied. I've had my arms twisted. I've been made to scream with pain in other ways. I've been flung into a filthy cell with a lot of other poor wretches as if I were a sack of coals being emptied into a cellar. And the only difference between me and the others was that I hit back. Yes I did. And I did worse. I wasn't ladylike. I cursed. I called names. I heard words that I didn't even know that I knew, coming out of my mouth just as if somebody else had spoken them. The policeman repeated them in court. The magistrate said he could hardly believe it. The policeman held out his hand with his two teeth in it that I knocked out. I said it was all right; that I had heard myself using those words quite distinctly; and that I had taken the good conduct prize for three years running at school. The poor old gentleman put me back for the missionary to find out who I was, and to ascertain the state of my mind. I wouldn't tell, of course, for your sakes at home here; and I wouldn't say I was sorry, or apologise to the policeman, or compensate him or anything of that sort. I wasn't sorry. The one thing that gave me any satisfaction was getting in that smack on his mouth; and I said so. So the missionary reported that I seemed hardened and that no doubt I would tell who I was after a day in prison. Then I was sentenced. So now you see I'm not a bit the sort of girl you thought me. I'm not a bit the sort of girl I thought myself. And I don't know what sort of person you really are, or what sort of person father really is. I wonder what he would say or do if he had an angry brute of a policeman twisting his arm with one hand and rushing him along by the nape of his neck with the other. He couldn't whirl his leg like a windmill and knock a policeman down by a glorious kick on the helmet. Oh, if they'd all fought as we two fought we'd have beaten them.

Lynn – 19

FLATMATES ELLEN DRYDEN

First workshopped and performed by the Chiswick Youth Theatre and published in 2000. The action takes place in a student flat in the 1990s.

Steve, a law student whose wealthy parents own the flat, rents out two rooms to **Lynn** and Tom, who are studying English. Steve is bored with Tom and tells **Lynn** that he has advertised his room. A music student is interested in taking it over and will be able to pay him more money. He wants **Lynn** to interview her. As **Lynn** starts to protest the doorbell rings and Steve shows in Coralie and her boyfriend, Tony. He then excuses himself and goes out, leaving the three of them together.

Lynn is fuming. She is in no mood to interview anyone. Finally Coralie asks if there is any point in her staying. Perhaps she should come back later when Steve and Tom are there?

From: *Six Primroses Each and other Plays for Young Actors*
Published by First Writes Publications, London

Lynn

I ought to say I'm sorry. But I'm not. Oh! Not you. I only heard about you a few minutes ago. Steve's little joke. He is a wealthy, spoilt brat who's only interested in his stomach. When he's not eating he pushes people around for fun. Tom is a raging neurotic with a chip on his shoulder, who is busy working himself into a really juicy breakdown. They fight. Incessantly. I spend as little time as possible here because both of them, in their different ways, cling to the sweet old-fashioned notion that – deep down – I am longing to do their washing and cooking for them, and I only refuse because I'm scared that the sisters' heavy mob will come and do me over if I give way to my natural instincts and start mothering them both. Steve is reading law – officially. Tom and I are both doing English. He always hands his work in on the dot. I don't even do the work. So tutorials are a permanent embarrassment specially as I'm brighter than he is. He tries to make me work – to fulfil my potential. I refuse. He manages to miss the point about absolutely every-thing. Life and Literature. And he is scared of girls. In case they don't measure up to Mummy. Steve's scared of them too. In case they don't take food seriously . . . If you think that's a calmer atmosphere than people 'having a relationship' as you call it – getting up at lunchtime, gazing into each others' eyes instead of lunch, then disappearing for the afternoon and going for long intense walks all evening – well, you're welcome to move in right now! Rent money in advance. Strict demarcation of the 'fridge. Steve has three quarters of it. The rest of us share the one remaining shelf. Gas meter. Immersion Heater. Telephone timer. Put your calls down in the book. Launderette down the road. Delicatessen and paper shop on the corner. No credit. The Dairy stopped delivering milk because we always managed to be out when he called to be paid. Or hid. Or didn't have the money in Tom's case. *(Pause)* Is that the sort of thing you were looking for?

Mabel Chiltern – young

AN IDEAL HUSBAND OSCAR WILDE

This society comedy was first performed in 1895 at the Haymarket Theatre and is set in fashionable London.

The 'Ideal Husband' of the title is Sir Robert Chiltern, Under Secretary for Foreign Affairs, who – having in his youth sold private information about a transaction contemplated by the Government of the day – is now being threatened with exposure by the unscrupulous Mrs Cheveley. He is saved from disgrace by the intervention of his friend, Lord Goring.

Mabel Chiltern is Sir Robert's high-spirited young sister, who throughout the play is being relentlessly pursued by her brother's secretary, Tommy Trafford, but finally accepts a proposal of marriage from Lord Goring.

In this scene, **Mabel** is complaining to her sister-in-law, Lady Chiltern, about Tommy's latest proposal. Lady Chiltern protests that Tommy is the best secretary her brother ever had. He has a brilliant future before him.

Published by New Mermaids

Mabel Chiltern

Gertrude, I wish you would speak to Tommy Trafford . . . Well, Tommy has proposed to me again. Tommy really does nothing but propose to me. He proposed to me last night in the music-room, when I was quite unprotected, as there was an elaborate trio going on. I didn't dare to make the smallest repartee, I need hardly tell you. If I had, it would have stopped the music at once. Musical people are so absurdly unreasonable. They always want one to be perfectly dumb at the very moment when one is longing to be absolutely deaf. Then he proposed to me in broad daylight this morning, in front of that dreadful statue of Achilles. Really, the things that go on in front of that work of art are quite appalling. The police should interfere. At luncheon I saw by the glare in his eye that he was going to propose again, and I just managed to check him in time by assuring him that I was a bimetallist. Fortunately I don't know what bimetallism means. And I don't believe anybody else does either. But the observation crushed Tommy for ten minutes. He looked quite shocked. And then Tommy is so annoying in the way he proposes. If he proposed at the top of his voice, I should not mind so much. That might produce some effect on the public. But he does it in a horrid confidential way. When Tommy wants to be romantic he talks to one just like a doctor. I am very fond of Tommy, but his methods of proposing are quite out of date. I wish, Gertrude, you would speak to him, and tell him that once a week is quite often enough to propose to anyone, and that it should always be done in a manner that attracts some attention . . . I must go round now and rehearse at Lady Basildon's. You remember we are having *tableaux*, don't you? The Triumph of something, I don't know what! I hope it will be triumph of me. Only triumph I am really interested in at present. *(Kisses* Lady Chiltern *and goes out; then comes running back)* Oh, Gertrude, do you know who is coming to see you? That dreadful Mrs Cheveley, in a most lovely gown. Did you ask her? . . . I assure you she is coming upstairs, as large as life and not nearly so natural.

Rena – 20s, Black American

JITNEY ANGUS WILSON

First produced at the Royal National Theatre in 2001 and set in a jitney station in Pittsburg, Pennsylvania, where a firm of cab drivers serves the black neighbourhoods.

The station is run by Becker, a well-respected man in his 60s. His drivers are Turbo, Fielding, Doub and Youngblood. Youngblood and his girlfriend, **Rena** are struggling to make a life for themselves and their young son. Youngblood is hardly ever at home and rumour has it he is running around with **Rena**'s sister, 'Peaches'.

In this scene **Rena** has called in at the station to confront Youngblood. He didn't come home last night and she demands to know where he was. She wants someone who's going to share with her, not hide things away from her. Youngblood tells her he has bought her a house and wanted to surprise her with it.

Published by Nick Hern Books, London

Rena

A house? A house, Darnell? You bought a house without me! . . . You gonna surprise me with a house? Don't do that. A new TV maybe. A stereo . . . a couch . . . a refrigerator . . . okay. But don't surprise me with a house that I didn't even have a chance to pick out! That's what you been doing? That's the debt you had to pay? . . . Darnell, you ain't bought no house without me. How many times in your life do you get to pick out a house? . . . Naw, you bought a den for Darnell . . . that's what you did. So you can sit down there and watch your football games. But what about the kitchen? The bathroom? How many windows does it have in the bedroom? Is there some place for Jesse to play? How much closet space does it have? You can't just surprise me with a house and I'm supposed to say, 'Oh, Darnell, that's nice.' At one time I would have. But I'm not 17 no more. I have responsibilities. I want to know if it has a hookup for a washer and dryer cause I got to wash Jesse's clothes. I want to know if it has a yard and do it have a fence and how far Jesse has to go to school. I ain't thinking about where to put the TV. That's not what's important to me. And you supposed to know, Darnell. You supposed to know what's important to me like I'm supposed to know what's important to you. I'm not asking you to do it by yourself. I'm here with you. We in this together. See . . . house or no house we still ain't got the food money. But if you had come and told me . . . if you had shared that with me . . . we could have went to my mother and we could have got 80 dollars for the house and still had money for food. You just did it all wrong, Darnell. I mean, you did the right thing but you did it wrong.

jitney   a small bus carrying passengers for a low fare.

Angela – Northern, 16

LIKE A VIRGIN GORDON STEEL

First performed by the Hull Truck Theatre Company at the Dovecote Arts Centre, Stockton-on-Tees, in 1995, at the Edinburgh Festival and then on a nationwide tour. It is set in Middlesborough.

Angela and her friend, Maxine, are besotted with Madonna. They play truant from school, form a band, have numerous boyfriends and dream of becoming famous very soon. Then Angela becomes unwell. The doctor diagnoses Myeloid Leukemia and she is put on chemotherapy. She is warned she may lose her hair and buys herself a Madonna-style wig. Maxine says it looks awful.

In this scene the girls are in Angela's bedroom. Maxine is ecstatic. Jamie Powers, the boy she's been crying her eyes out over, has phoned her and, what's more, invited her back to his house while his mam and dad are out. She wants to go down the pub and celebrate, but Angela doesn't feel like it. Maxine tells her to stop feeling sorry for herself – it's difficult but she has to make the most of it. She must get out and try to live a bit.

Published by Oberon Books, London
The full text is currently available from Oberon Books, ISBN: 1840021403.

Angela

No, you go. I don't feel up to it . . . I've got to live a bit. Maxine, I'm dying. I don't know why but I am. I don't know why I've been picked to have such a shit-awful life. What have I done that's so bloody wrong? So you can piss off with your, 'Let's be jolly,' routine. With your, 'Let's pretend everything's alright and we'll have a laugh like we used to in the old days.' . . . Do you know something? *(Pause)* I've never had sex. I'm a virgin. Yeah I know what I said, what we said, but . . . well, they were just stories full of me, us trying to be grown-up. But I'm not gonna grow up. I'll never grow up and be a woman and have children. Why me? Why the fucking hell does it have to be me? It's not fair. How would you feel if someone told you that you were gonna die? Come on, it's not easy is it? YOU ARE GOING TO DIE. You have got four weeks to live. What are you going to do? *(Pause)* It's not easy, is it, and people are so full of understanding . . . so full of shit. 'I'd go on holiday, I'd travel.' What is the point in spending your time in strange lands with strange people? So you'll have lots of happy memories and photographs to look back on. When? I haven't got time, I'm dying. What's the point in laying on a beach getting a tan? So I'll look good in my coffin. So people will be able to gork into my coffin with . . . with . . . tear-stained eyes and say . . . 'She looks really good' . . . 'She's the best suntanned corpse I've ever seen' . . . Well, they can all fuck off. Sometimes I feel as though I should have dignity and write poems and raise money for charity an' all that . . . Be a symbol for other people to look up to. But why should I? What has anybody ever done for me? Look at you, you're pathetic stood there not wanting to say anything in case you hurt my feelings. Making excuses for me. 'It's her condition . . . It's understandable . . . She's just a bit down.' Well don't patronise me. Tell me to fuck off. Slap me. Go on. *(She pushes* Maxine*)* Go on. *(She pushes her again)* Go on, do something.

Girleen – Irish/Galway, 17

THE LONESOME WEST MARTIN MCDONAGH

Presented at the Royal Court Theatre in 1997 as part of the Leenane Trilogy and set in Leenane, Galway.

Two brothers, Coleman and Valene, live side by side in an old farmhouse. They are forever quarrelling, even becoming violent as the poteen – supplied to them by **Girleen**'s father – takes hold of them. A young priest, Father Welsh, unable to cope with the slaughtering and suicide among his parishioners, also finds solace in drink. He tries to settle the differences between the two brothers but it's a hopeless task. And they in turn try to cheer him up by pointing out the good he has done in the parish. Even **Girleen** does her best to joke him out of his 'crisis of faith'. After all, he does train the 'under-twelves' – a notoriously rough girls' football team.

In this scene Father Welsh is sitting on a bench on a lakeside jetty at night. He has just come back from conducting the funeral service for Tom Hanlon who drowned himself in the lake. He has a pint in his hand. **Girleen** enters. She sits down beside him. She congratulates him on his sermon and he tells her he is leaving the parish.

Published by Dramatists Play Service, Inc.

Girleen

Father. What are ya up to? . . . That was a nice sermon at Thomas's today, Father . . . I was at the back a ways. *(Pause)* Almost made me go crying, them words did . . . I'd be saying you've had a few now, Father? . . . I wasn't starting on ya . . . I wasn't starting at all on ya. I do tease you sometimes but that's all I do do . . . I do only tease you now and again, and only to camouflage the mad passion I have deep within me for ya . . . *(Welsh gives her a dirty look. She smiles)* No, I'm only joking now, Father . . . Ah be taking a joke will ya, Father? It's only cos you're so high-horse and up yourself that you make such an easy target . . . It's tonight you're going? . . . But that's awful quick. No one'll have a chance to wish you good-bye, Father . . . Will you write to me from where you're going and be giving me your new address, Father . . . Just so's we can say hello now and then, now . . . It's more than Thomas has killed himself here down the years, d'you know, Father? Three other fellas walked in here, me mam was telling me . . . You're not scared because you're pissed to the gills. I'm not scared because . . . I don't know why. One, because you're here, and two, because . . . I don't know. I don't be scared of cemeteries at night either. The opposite of that, I do like cemeteries at night . . . *(Embarrassed throughout)* It's because . . . even if you're sad or something, or lonely or something, you're still better off than them lost in the ground or in the lake, because . . . at least you've got the *chance* of being happy, and even if it's a real little chance, it's more than them dead ones have. And it's not that you're saying, 'Hah, I'm better than ye,' no, because in the long run it might end up that you have a worse life than ever they had and you'd've been better off as dead as them, there and then. But at least when you're still here there's the *possibility* of happiness, and it's like them dead ones know that, and they're happy for you to have it. They say 'Good luck to ya.' *(Quietly)* Is the way I see it anyways . . . I'll be carrying on the road home for meself now, Father. Will you be staying or will you be walking with me? . . . See you so, Father . . . If you let me know where you get to I'll write with how the under-twelves get on tomorrow. It may be in the *Tribune* anyways. Under 'Girl decapitated in football match'.

Sally – 20

LOVE ON THE DOLE
RONALD GOW AND WALTER GREENWOOD

First performed at the Manchester Repertory Theatre in 1934 and in London at the Garrick Theatre in 1935, it is set in Hanky Park, Salford, Lancashire.

In Hanky Park in the 1930s, unemployment is high. The Hardcastles are a respectable working-class family. But Mr Hardcastle is on the dole, his wife takes in washing and their son, Harry, works in a machine shop for a few shillings a week. Only their daughter **Sally**, who works in the local mill, brings in a proper wage.

Sally meets and falls in love with Larry Meath and they plan to get married and move away from Hanky Park. When he is killed during a riot at a street-meeting her hopes and plans for a better future are shattered. She becomes the mistress of Sam Grundy, a prosperous bookmaker and her father turns her out of the house.

In this scene **Sally** is dressed for her departure. She carries a small leather suitcase. Her father demands to know if the tales he's heard about her are true.

Published by Samuel French, London

Sally

It's true, Mother, and I don't care who knows it. *(She crosses to R of the table)* Aye, and I'll tell you something else. It's sick I am of codging old clothes to try and make them look like something. And sick I am of working week after week and seeing nothing for it. I'm sick of never having anything but what's been in pawnshops and crawling with vermin – oh, I'm sick of the sight of Hanky Park and everybody in it . . . Who cares what folk say? There's none I know as wouldn't swap places with me if they had the chance. You'd have me wed, would you? Then tell me where's the fellow around here can afford it. Them as *is* working ain't able to keep themselves, never mind a wife. Look at yourself – and look at our Harry! On workhouse relief and ain't even got a bed as he can call his own. I suppose I'd be fit to call your daughter if I was like that with a tribe of kids at me skirts. Well, can you get our Harry a job? No, but I can. Yes, me. I've got influence now – but I'm not respectable . . . *(She crosses to the sofa, picks up her jacket and puts it on then turns to face her father)* You kicked our Harry out because he got married and you're kicking me out because I ain't. You'd have me like all the rest of the women, working themselves to death and getting nothing for it. Look at Mother! Look at her! *(Pointing)* Well there ain't a man breathing, now Larry's gone, who can get me like *that* – for him!

97

Frankie – American, 12

MEMBER OF THE WEDDING
CARSON MCCULLERS

First produced in New York in 1950 at the Empire Theatre and set in a small southern town in America in August 1945. **Frankie** is a dreamy, restless girl – one moment full of energy and the next, retreating into her fantasy world. She adores her brother Jarvis and his fiancée Janice, who are soon to be married, and has made up her mind that after the wedding she will stay with them and they will all three travel the world together. She confides her dreams to Berenice, the black cook, who warns her that two is company and three is a crowd, especially at weddings.

In this scene **Frankie** wanders out into the yard. Berenice has gone out for the evening with friends, and **Frankie** feels excluded. She calls across to her little cousin John Henry to come over and spend the night with her. John Henry wants to go out and play with the other children, but **Frankie** only wants to talk about the wedding. She is restless and disturbed.

A *New Directions* Paperback

Frankie

I told Berenice that I was leavin' town for good and she did not believe me. Sometimes I honestly think she is the biggest fool that ever drew breath. You try to impress something on a big fool like that, and it's just like talking to a block of cement. I kept on telling and telling and telling her. I told her I had to leave this town for good because it is inevitable. Inevitable . . . Don't bother me, John Henry. I'm thinking . . . About the wedding. About my brother and the bride. Everything's been so sudden today. I never believed before about the fact that the earth turns at the rate of about a thousand miles a day. I didn't understand why it was that if you jumped up in the air you wouldn't land in Selma or Fairview or somewhere else instead of the same back yard. But now it seems to me I feel the world going around very fast. *(Frankie begins turning around in circles with arms outstretched. John Henry copies her. They both turn)* I feel it turning and it makes me dizzy . . . *(Suddenly stopping her turning)* I just now thought of something . . . I know where I'm going . . . I tell you I know where I'm going. It's like I've known it all my life. Tomorrow I will tell everybody . . . *(Dreamily)* After the wedding I'm going with them to Winter Hill. I'm going off with them after the wedding . . . Shush, just now I realised something. The trouble with me is that for a long time I have been just an 'I' person. All other people can say 'we'. When Berenice says 'we' she means her lodge and church and coloured people. Soldiers can say 'we' and mean the army. All people belong to a 'we' except me . . . Not to belong to a 'we' makes you too lonesome. Until this afternoon I didn't have a 'we', but now after seeing Janice and Jarvis I suddenly realise something . . . I know that the bride and my brother are the 'we' of me. So I'm going with them, and joining with the wedding. This coming Sunday when my brother and the bride leave this town, I'm going with the two of them to Winter Hill. And after that to whatever place that they will ever go. *(There is a pause)* I love the two of them so much and we belong to be together. I love the two of them so much because they are the *we* of me.

Mercy – young

MERCY FINE SHELLEY SILAS

First produced for Clean Break – an education and new writing company, opening their Autumn Tour at the Birmingham Repertory Theatre and transferring to the Southwark Playhouse in November 2005.

Mercy Fine is of mixed blood: her father was black and her mother, white. She is spending her last day in an open prison where she has just completed a life sentence for murdering her mother's partner. In 24 hours she will be going back home – but home was where everything went so tragically wrong.

In this scene she is talking to her friend Viv, who has arranged a farewell celebration for her. We also see flashbacks of her mother, sitting at the kitchen table talking to her. It is confession time – and **Mercy** confesses to Viv that she was innocent and took the blame for her mentally frail mother.

Published by Oberon Modern Plays, London
The full text is currently available from Oberon Books, ISBN: 1840026375.

Mercy

I'm not a violent person . . . *(Beat.)* You know, she was the sweetest, most generous . . . she would get up at six, make coffee for him so it was hot when he woke up. She had a bath and put on her make-up, because he said he didn't want to look at an ugly cow in the morning or smell her night-time smell. She wore thick mascara and painted her lips so they were bright. And she walked quietly around the place, so she didn't disturb him. And I'd listen, and watch, as she walked around her home like it belonged to someone else. Like it belonged to him. Because that's how he used to act. Like he owned the place. Like fuck he did. He used to treat her like shit. Like a dog. And I had to watch. If he didn't like something she cooked for him, he'd throw it in the bin. If we were having dinner or watching TV, and he wanted to have sex, he'd click his fingers at me and I'd have to go outside and wait. And wait. So I'd go down the chip shop, get some chocolate. Keep me warm and wired. And he played music. All the time. That fucking music, made me mad. And his mouth, his mouth said words no one should say, words that no one should hear. He said a white woman needed a white man, not a man like my father. He said I was like washing that hadn't been rinsed out. I was like a stain. A big stain . . . She had this china. Best plates we could have eaten off. From her mum. Proper china plates. You know. Blue and white. With a shine on them. *(Beat.)* He smashed them, one at a time. In front of her. When he'd gone she picked up all the pieces . . . I could never understand why we stayed on, why we let him do what he did.

Frehia – Asian, young

MERCY FINE SHELLEY SILAS

First produced for Clean Break – an education and new writing company, opening their Autumn Tour at the Birmingham Repertory Theatre and transferring to Southwark Playhouse in November 2005.

It is Mercy Fine's last day in an open prison where she has just completed a life sentence for murder. Her friends, Viv and **Frehia** are preparing a farewell celebration for her. **Frehia** is subject to mood swings and describes herself as bi-polar, disturbed, juxtaposed – but like Viv, she is fond of Mercy and will miss her when she leaves.

In this scene **Frehia** enters with a Sainsbury's bag. She has bought Mercy a birthday cake. Mercy has been sent for by the Governor and Viv is anxious about her . . .

Published by Oberon Modern Plays, London
The full text is currently available from Oberon Books, ISBN: 1840026375.

Frehia

Mercy in here? . . . Governor wants to see you . . . He's got a right face on him. What have you done now, Mercy Fine?

Mercy sighs and exits and stands outside the Governor's office. Frehia looks around the room, at the decorations.

Frehia removes a box from the plastic bag. It's a Spongebob Square Pants Happy Birthday cake.

A cake . . . It is her birthday, sort of. From tomorrow it'll be like she's reborn. Inshallah! . . . She's fine. Governor's probably giving her a talk, you know, remember everything you've learned in here, remember to be an upstanding member of the community, remember that we care about you. Remember that this is a journey, and we're all on it together. We're in the driving seat, and you're a passenger, but when you leave here it's the other way around. Except Mercy is a driver, isn't she, she drives people around, so she's the driver. I don't drive any more. I'm driven. Remember, Mercy Fine, remember. Don't ever forget or you'll end up back here . . . Heard it last time I was in. *(Beat.)* And the time before. Sometimes, they give you a talk, a mini lecture. Makes them feel good. Makes them feel they've achieved something. Like they've done you this big fuck-off favour. But the last thing you want the night before you get out is some middle-aged bloke poking a finger at you, smiling and telling you how you should and shouldn't behave. Remember, remember, never forget or you'll be back. Society is on the lookout for your kind. Oh yeah, what's my kind? . . . I know, I talk too much. I talk to everyone. All the time. I'm troubled. Disturbed. Juxtaposed. What is it they call me? Bi-polar. It's not my fault. It's just the way I was born. Some people are born good. Some people are born like me. Not good not bad. Just inconvenienced. It's in my genes, you know. You know, in here.

Rachel - 20

NATHAN THE WISE
GOTTHOLD EPHRAIM LESSING
A VERSION BY EDWARD KEMP

This revival of a German classic was first performed at the Minerva Theatre, Chichester in 2003 and transferred to The Hampstead Theatre, London in 2005. Set in Jerusalem in 1192, it is a plea for religious tolerance.

   Rachel is the daughter of Nathan, a rich Jew who is liked and respected by everyone. He has just returned home to learn that his daughter has been involved in a terrible fire, but was miraculously rescued by an angel. Daya, the Christian woman who has bought **Rachel** up from a child, explains that her 'angel was a Knight Templar'. **Rachel** refuses to believe her: there are no Templars left in Jerusalem.

Published by Nick Hern Books, London

Rachel

Father. Is it really you? I thought I must have dreamt your voice. Well? What mountains and rivers lie between us now? Here we stand breathing the same air, and you don't rush to embrace me. I was in a fire. I nearly died. Don't tremble. It was only nearly. Fire is a terrible way to die . . . You had to cross the Euphrates, the Tigris, the Jordan – all those rivers – I used to worry about you so much before the fire came. But now I think how wonderful it must be to die in water, how cooling, how welcoming. No, you're not drowned and I'm not burnt. We should rejoice and praise God. He bore you over the waters on the wings of invisible angels. But I saw my angel, he carried me out of the fire on his white wings . . . I saw them. I saw him as plainly as I see you . . . He didn't *seem* like an angel, he was one . . . Who taught me that angels exist? That they hover around us at all times? And that God sends them to work miracles for those who love Him. And I've loved Him haven't I? . . . That proves it, don't you see. It couldn't possibly have been a real Templar, because what could a Templar be doing in Jerusalem? He only *seemed* to be one, but actually he was an angel . . . and how could a Templar vanish into thin air?

Carol – young, American

OLEANNA DAVID MAMET

First performed at the Orpheum Theatre, New York in 1992 and at the Royal Court Theatre in 1993, transferring to the Duke of York's Theatre, London later that year.

A dramatised power struggle in three acts, it has been described as a 'furious probing of power politics, sexual harassment hysteria, ideological agendas and so-called political correctness'.

The action takes place in university professor John's office, where he is confronted by one of his students, **Carol**, who supposedly has come to talk to him about her grades. Their discussion is repeatedly interrupted by telephone calls from John's wife. He is distracted, fails to really listen to what **Carol** is saying to him and cannot understand why she needs to take notes during their conversation. She grows more and more agitated and he attempts to calm her by placing his hands on her shoulders. She storms out of the office.

A month later John is informed that the 'Group' that **Carol** represents has approached his 'tenure' committee and he is being charged with sexual harassment. He stands to lose his job and will no longer be able to complete the purchase on his new home.

In this scene, John has invited **Carol** to his office to explain why she has done this. She hands him her report. Her allegations are obviously false; however, she has taken notes of their previous conversation and presented them word for word, but completely out of context, to the committee.

Published by Methuen, London

Note: the title *Oleanna* is taken from an American folk song, 'Oh to be in Oleanna – that's where I would rather be/Than be bound in Norway and drag the chains of slavery.'

Carol

I don't *care* what you think . . . Professor. I came here as a *favour*. At your personal request. Perhaps I should not have done so . . . What gives you the *right*. Yes. To speak to a *woman* in your private . . . Yes. Yes. I'm sorry. I'm sorry. You feel yourself empowered . . . you say so, yourself. To *strut*. To *posture*. To 'perform'. To 'call me in here. . .' Eh? You say that higher education is a joke. And treat it as such, you *treat* it as such. And *confess* to a taste to play the *Patriarch* in your class. To grant *this*. To deny *that*. To embrace your students . . . How can you *deny* it. You did it to me. *Here*. You *did* . . . You *confess*. You love the Power. To *deviate*. To *invent*, to transgress . . . to *transgress* whatever norms have been established, for us. And you think it's charming to 'question' in yourself this taste to mock and destroy. But you should question it, Professor. And you pick those things which you feel *advance* you: publication, *tenure*, and the steps to get them you call 'harmless rituals'. And you perform those steps. Although you say it is hypocrisy. But to the aspirations of your students. Of *hardworking students*, who come here, who *slave* to come here – you have no idea what it cost me to come to this school – you *mock* us. You call education 'hazing', and from your so-protected, so-elitist seat you hold our confusion as a *joke*, and our hopes and efforts with it. Then you sit there and say, 'What have I done?' And ask me to understand that *you* have aspirations too. But I tell you. I tell you. that you are vile. And that you are exploitative. And if you possess one ounce of that inner honesty you describe in your book, you can look in yourself and see those things that I see. And you can find revulsion equal to my own. Good day. *[She prepares to leave the room.]*

Mary Mooney – 15–16

ONCE A CATHOLIC MARY O'MALLEY

First performed at the Royal Court Theatre in 1977 and set in the Convent of Our Lady of Fatima – a Grammar School for Girls – and in and around the streets of Willesden and Harlesden, London NW10, from September 1956 to July 1957.

Mary Mooney is a fifth-former, plain and rather scruffy but with a good singing voice. Her ambition is to become a nun. In this scene she is walking down the street with Mary McGinty and Mary Gallaher. All three are carrying heavy satchels and eating Mars Bars. Mary McGinty has refused to wear her hat and Mary Gallaher warns her that if a prefect sees her she'll get reported. McGinty doesn't care. It wouldn't worry her if she got expelled. She wonders what she'd have to do to get expelled from 'that old dump'. Perhaps she could 'make a big long willy out of plasticine and stick it on the crucifix in the chapel'. Mary Mooney is shocked – McGinty mustn't say things like that.

[McGINTY: 'Why not? Do you reckon a thunderbolt is gonna come hurtling down from Heaven?']

Published by Amber Lane Press, Charlbury, Oxfordshire

Mary Rooney

You mustn't say things like that . . . It doesn't happen straight away. It happens when you're least expecting it. You'd better make an Act of Contrition . . . My Dad knows this man who used to be a monk. But he couldn't keep his vows so he asked if he could be released. On the day he left he came skipping down the path with his collar in his hand. And when he opened the monastery gate he saw an alsatian sitting outside. So he hung his collar round the alsatian's neck and went on his way laughing all along the road. After that he started going into pubs every night and boasting to all the people about what he'd gone and done with his collar. Then one day he went and got married. And while he was on his honeymoon he started to get a really bad pain in his back. He was in such a terrible agony he could only walk about with a stoop. And after a while he was completely bent up double. Then he started to lose his voice. He went to loads of different doctors but none of them could do anything to help him. And now he can only get about on all fours. And when he opens his mouth to say anything he barks just like a dog. Of course it's true. He lives in Shepherds Bush . . . I bet if you were knocked down by a trolley bus this evening you'd be yelling your head off for a priest.

Sally Stokes – 17

THE PASSING-OUT PARADE ANNE VALERY

First presented at the Greenwich Theatre in 1979 and set in an ATS Barrack Room in Pontefract, Yorkshire, in early 1944.

A new group of ATS girls have arrived at the barracks. Over the next few weeks it is Sergeant Pickering's job to turn these raw recruits into 'a first class war machine' for the Passing-Out Parade. **Private Sally Stokes** is one of these recruits. The eldest of a large Catholic family, she was physically abused by her father and sent to a Children's Home. She takes her religion seriously and is upset by any irreverent references to 'God' and 'Christ'. The mention of sex also upsets her.

In this scene the girls are drinking cider and singing bawdy songs. **Stokes** has just been sick. It is her 'first time boozing'. Private Crab leads her to a chair and sits her down. She hands her a bottle of cider, telling her to take a swig: 'Hair of the dog – it helps.'

Stokes starts to read aloud the letter she has received from Reverend Mother at the Home. Then, because she is slightly drunk, she begins to talk about her Mum and we get a glimpse of her life before she was sent away.

Published by Samuel French, London

Note: The letter from Reverend Mother is an addition from the next scene, as **Stokes**'s following speech is a little too short for most auditions.

Stokes

[Sits at the table and reads her letter] 'Dear Child, Your mother has asked me to write this letter for her. She wishes to thank you for the ten shillings and to tell you she lit a candle to our Blessed Lady. You'll be sorry to hear that The Home was hit, though the good Lord saw fit to spare us. Minnie Simpson – who I believe was a special friend of yours – is now working at your old job as scullery maid. She sends the enclosed handkerchief, which she embroidered in the rest period. We all pray for you daily, that you may remain in the path of obedience in which you were raised. May God keep you. Reverend Mother. PS Father O'Brian wishes to remind you of the penance you were given.' *[She strokes the handkerchief, in tears]* . . . Me mum's a Catholic . . . *[Talking because she is drunk]* She's a proper Catholic. Don't never drink nor smoke nor swear. And she takes us to Mass – in clean socks! 'Cepting Dad of course. Says he's drinking for rest, he does. *[She hiccups]* Of a Saturday night he'd come home – you know . . . *[She looks at Crab]* Mum in with us, 'case he were too gone to notice. We'd lie there for hours sometimes – ever so still – even baby, waiting for his sound on the stair. And when he got by our door, we'd go all – little. *[She makes a gesture, crouching]* Even our mum . . . *[At Crab, scared]* Bang! *[She puts her hand to her ear]* Bang'd go the door 'gainst the dresser, mirror swinging – so we'd sees ourselves – all arms and bits – and Dad falling in shouting, 'Let's be 'aving you.' I looks through my fingers once, and he were so – so *big*! And then – sudden like – he'd – yank Mum out. Drag her all way 'cross the lino, and her clinging on to things and crying out to the Blessed Virgin to spare her. She never did. *[Closes her eyes and lies back]*.

Eliza Doolittle – 18/20

PYGMALION GEORGE BERNARD SHAW

A romantic comedy first produced in German in Vienna in 1913 and then in London the following year. It was the source of a successful American musical, *My Fair Lady*, in 1956 – seen most recently at the Royal National Theatre in 2001.

Professor Henry Higgins, a professor of phonetics, boasts to his friend Colonel Pickering, that he could pass a cockney flower girl off as a duchess by teaching her to speak properly. The girl, **Eliza Doolittle**, calls at Higgins' house and asks him to give her lessons. He takes her on as his pupil and she finally emerges not only as a 'lady' but also as a beautiful and sensitive woman.

In this scene Higgins has invited **Liza** to his mother's at-home day. Henry promises Mrs Higgins that she has strict orders as to her behaviour and has been told to stick to two subjects, the weather and everybody's health. Mrs Eynsford Hill and her daughter are the first to arrive, followed by Colonel Pickering and Freddie Eynsford Hill. When **Liza** makes her entrance she is exquisitely dressed and speaks with pedantic correctness. Mrs Higgins opens the conversation by commenting on the weather, to which Mrs Eynsford Hill replies that she hopes it won't turn cold as there's so much influenza about.

Published by Penguin Books, London

Liza

The shallow depression in the west of these islands is likely to move slowly in an easterly direction. There are no indications of any great change in the barometrical situation . . . What is wrong with that, young man? I bet I got it right . . . *(darkly)* My aunt died of influenza: so they said. *(In the same tragic tone)* But it's my belief they done the old woman in . . . Y-e-e-e-es, Lord love you! Why should she die of influenza? She come through diphtheria right enough the year before. I saw her with my own eyes. Fairly blue with it, she was. They all thought she was dead: but my father he kept ladling gin down her throat til she came to so sudden that she bit the bowl off the spoon . . . *(piling up the indictment)* What call would a woman with that strength in her have to die of influenza? What become of her new straw hat that should have come to me? Somebody pinched it; and what I say is, them as pinched it done her in . . . Them she lived with would have killed her for a hat-pin, let alone a hat . . . Gin was mother's milk to her. Besides, he'd poured so much down his own throat that he knew the good of it . . . It never did him no harm what I could see but then he did not keep it up regular. *(Cheerfully)* On the burst, as you might say, from time to time. And always more agreeable when he had a drop in. When he was out of work, my mother used to give him fourpence and tell him to go out and not come back until he'd drunk himself cheerful and loving-like. There's lots of women has to make their husbands drunk to make them fit to live with. *(Now quite at her ease)* You see, it's like this. If a man has a bit of a conscience, it always takes him when he's sober; and then it makes him low-spirited. A drop of booze just takes that off and makes him happy. *(To Freddy, who is in convulsions of suppressed laughter)* Here! what are you sniggering at? . . . If I was doing it proper, what was you laughing at? *(To Higgins)* Have I said anything I oughtn't?

Lucy – 17 or 18

THE RIVALS RICHARD BRINSLEY SHERIDAN

First produced at Covent Garden in 1775 and most recently by the Royal Shakespeare Company at the Barbican in 2000.

Lydia Languish, a wealthy young heiress, is staying with her aunt, Mrs Malaprop, in Bath. She is in love with a penniless junior officer, Ensign Beverley, of whom her aunt heartily disapproves. Meanwhile Mrs Malaprop herself is involved in an exchange of amorous correspondence with an Irish Baronet, Sir Lucius O'Trigger. Lydia's maid **Lucy**, a crafty young woman out to make a quick profit wherever she can, has been carrying the letters to and from Sir Lucius and has led him to believe that he is in fact corresponding with Lydia.

In this scene Mrs Malaprop calls for **Lucy** to take yet another letter to Sir Lucius. She warns her that being a 'simpleton' will not excuse any betrayal of confidence. Left alone, **Lucy** advises all girls of 'her station' to put on a mask of 'silliness', and recounts the inventory of the profits made by her 'simplicity'.

Published by New Mermaids

Lucy

Ha! ha! ha! So, my dear *simplicity*, let me give you a little respite – *(altering her manner)* let girls in my station be as fond as they please of appearing expert, and knowing in their trusts; commend me to a mask of silliness, and a pair of sharp eyes for my own interest under it! Let me see to what account I have turned my *simplicity* lately – *(looks at a paper)* For abetting Miss Lydia Languish in a design of running away with an ensign – in money – sundry times – twelve pound twelve – gowns, five – hats, ruffles, caps, etc, etc – numberless! From the said Ensign, within this last month, six guineas and a half – about a quarter's pay! Item, from Mrs Malaprop, for betraying the young people to her – when I found matters were likely to be discovered – two guineas, and a black paduasoy. Item, from Mr Acres, for carrying divers letters – which I never delivered – two guineas, and a pair of buckles. Item, from Sir Lucius O'Trigger – three crowns – two gold pocket-pieces – and a silver snuff-box! – Well done, *simplicity*! – yet I was forced to make my Hibernian believe, that he was corresponding, not with the aunt, but with the niece: for, though not over rich, I found he had too much pride and delicacy to sacrifice the feelings of a gentleman to the necessities of his fortune.

paduasoy	heavy corded silk; a gown of that material
divers	various
crowns	five-shilling pieces
pocket-pieces	coins no longer current, or similar small objects, carried as lucky charms
Hibernian	Irishman

Juliet – 14

ROMEO AND JULIET WILLIAM SHAKESPEARE

A tragedy written in or around 1595, and set in Verona, it is the story of two 'star-crossed lovers', Romeo Montague and **Juliet Capulet**, whose tragic deaths end their families' long-standing feud.

    Juliet's father has arranged a grand feast in which she is to meet Paris, a young man who has asked for her hand in marriage. But by the end of the evening **Juliet** has met and fallen in love with Romeo, the son of the hated Montagues. The enmity between the two families makes it impossible for them to be together and so Romeo persuades Friar Lawrence to marry them secretly at his cell.

    Juliet has taken her Nurse into her confidence and sends her off early in the morning with a message for Romeo. In this scene she is waiting impatiently for her to return.

Published by Penguin Books, London

Juliet

The clock struck nine when I did send the Nurse.
In half an hour she promised to return.
Perchance she cannot meet him. That's not so.
O, she is lame! Love's heralds should be thoughts,
Which ten times faster glides than the sun's beams
Driving back shadows over louring hills.
Therefore do nimble-pinioned doves draw love,
And therefore hath the wind-swift Cupid wings.
Now is the sun upon the highmost hill
Of this day's journey, and from nine till twelve
Is three long hours, yet she is not come.
Had she affections and warm youthful blood,
She would be as swift in motion as a ball.
My words would bandy her to my sweet love,
And his to me.
But old folks, many feign as they were dead –
Unwieldy, slow, heavy and pale as lead.

(Enter Nurse *and* Peter*)*

O God, she comes! O honey Nurse, what news?
Hast thou met with him? Send thy man away.

Charlie – 15

SCHOOL PLAY SUZY ALMOND

First produced at the Soho Theatre, London, in 2001.

Charlie Silver is bad news in the South London comprehensive school: a problem to teachers and a bad influence on the rest of the class. Her ambitions are to front a gang, ride a motorbike and to 'mess with teachers' heads'. She boasts a long list of teachers who have given up on her account. Then Miss Fry, the new music teacher, arrives and things begin to change. **Charlie** is given countless detentions, but unknown to her 'gang' is using these detention periods to develop her suppressed musical talents.

In this scene **Charlie** is at the piano waiting for Miss Fry to arrive when her friend Lee comes bursting in. He accuses her of letting him down. She was supposed to meet him and Paul in the car park earlier that afternoon with her customised Hollister bike on which he was to ride 'a lap of honour' against his rival, Danny Chapel. **Charlie** says she has a music exam the next day and needs to practise. She tries to explain to him what playing the piano means to her and how Miss Fry has changed her way of thinking – not only about the music, but also about herself.

Published by Oberon Books, London
The full text is currently available from Oberon Books, ISBN: 184002237X.

Charlie

When you do something you don't have to be the best. If everyone thought like that, there wouldn't be any buses, cos . . . cos all the bus drivers would want a Gold medal every time they pulled out the station . . . Not bus drivers . . . I mean no-one would dare look at the stars in case someone goes 'Think you're an astronaut?' . . . Miss Fry says . . . *(Pause)* You've gotta understand . . . that I gave her a hard time for ages, I was so under her skin. A few years ago she got pissed up with all the bands, I thought – yeah I'll hang out with you . . . She was mental . . . She . . . One lesson . . . you see, some lessons she didn't actually teach. And sometimes, especially at the beginning, what she did was boring, you don't wanna hear, she drones. But now and again . . . One time she was about to play a song about a lady who drowned in a river, but it was nothing to do with the lesson, it was just that she liked it. I said it sounds miserable to me, miss, but she said hang on, and she told me the story: It's a sad song, she said . . . she fought for love and she lost . . . and now her skin is white as a lily, her lips are rose red, she's still and she floats downstream. She told me to close my eyes and imagine it was a dark moonlit night and that the water was lapping around the lady, taking her in. She said that when she got to the bridge of the song there would be a special note that didn't sound like the rest of the tune. It was a high sound, extra sad, a black key near the end of the piano – and when I heard it I had to imagine it was like a shooting star bursting across the river, trying to wake up the lady. I told her I couldn't be bothered, but when she started to play . . . And at the end of the second verse, when she hit that key and the sound broke, I felt the note shoot through the roof of this room like a bullet and I saw the star burst and I wanted the lady to wake up. I couldn't wait for that note to come around again. So that she'd open her eyes.

Heavenly – Southern American, young

SWEET BIRD OF YOUTH TENNESSEE WILLIAMS

First presented at the Martin Beck Theatre, New York, in 1959.

Chance Wayne is an ambitious hustler. He has currently taken up with the Princess Kosmonopolis, a fading film star, whom he imagines will be able to further his film career. She accompanies him back to his home town, where he attempts to see **Heavenly** with whom he once had an affair and still loves. But, unknown to him, he has infected her with venereal disease and her father, politician Boss Finley, has sworn to have him castrated.

Chance has been trying desperately to contact **Heavenly** – driving past her house in his car and making innumerable phone calls. In this scene Boss tells his daughter he wants to have a word with her. People are talking about her – she is becoming an issue, a subject of scandal – and this could harm his political career. In turn she accuses him of sending away the boy she loved, and reminds him that his well-known affair with the notorious 'Miss Lucy' has been going on even while her mother was still alive. He denies all knowledge of this. He wants her to go out and buy herself a brand new outfit and appear on the platform with him when he addresses the 'Youth for Tom Finley' club, in 'the stainless white of a virgin' to put an end to the ugly rumours that are going around about her.

Published by Penguin Books, London

Heavenly

Don't give me your 'Voice of God' speech. Papa, there was a time when you could have saved me, by letting me marry a boy that was still young and clean, but instead you drove him away, drove him out of St Cloud. And when he came back, you took me out of St Cloud, and tried to force me to marry a fifty-year-old money bag that you wanted something out of – . . . and then another, another, all of them ones that you wanted something out of. I'd gone, so Chance went away. Tried to compete, make himself big as these big-shots you wanted to use me for a bond with. He went. He tried. The right doors wouldn't open, and so he went in the wrong ones, and – Papa, you married for love, why wouldn't you let me do it, while I was alive, inside, and the boy still clean, still decent? . . . *(Shouting)* You married for love, but you wouldn't let me do it, and even though you'd done it, you broke Mama's heart, Miss Lucy had been your mistress – . . . Oh, Papa, she was your mistress long before Mama died. And Mama was just a front for you. Can I go in now, Papa? Can I go in now? . . . Papa, I'm sorry my operation has brought this embarrassment on you, but can you imagine it, Papa? I felt worse than embarrassed when I found out that Dr George Scudder's knife had cut the youth out of my body, made me an old childless woman. Dry, cold, empty, like an old woman. I feel as if I ought to rattle like a dead dried-up vine when the Gulf Wind blows, but, Papa – I won't embarrass you any more. I've made up my mind about something. If they'll let me, accept me, I'm going into a convent.

Ruby – Yorkshire, 16–17

WHEN WE ARE MARRIED J B PRIESTLEY

First performed at the St Martin's Theatre, London, in 1938 and most recently at the Haymarket Theatre in 1995.

The action takes place in the sitting room of Alderman Helliwell's house in Clecklewyke, a town in the West Riding, on an evening in 1908.

In this opening scene the front-door bell rings and **Ruby Birtle**, a very young 'slavey' of the period, shows in Gerald Forbes. Gerald has come to see Alderman Helliwell, but **Ruby** informs him he will have to wait. Alderman and Mrs Helliwell have company and they haven't finished their tea yet. Gerald is in no mood for a chat but **Ruby** insists on telling him all about the guests and every detail of what they are eating.

Published by Samuel French, London

Ruby

(L of the door) You'll have to wait, 'cos they haven't finished their tea
. . . *(Approaching, confidentially)* It's a do . . . A do. Y'know, they've
company . . . *(After nodding, going closer still)* Roast pork, stand pie,
salmon and salad, trifle, two kinds o' jellies, lemon-cheese tarts, jam tarts,
swiss tarts, sponge cake, walnut cake, chocolate roll, and a pound cake
kept from last Christmas . . . *(Seriously)* No, there's white bread, brown
bread, currant teacake, one o' them big curd tarts from Gregory's, and
a lot o' cheese . . . *(After nodding, then very confidentially)* And a little
brown jug . . . *(Still confidentially)* You know what that is, don't you?
(She laughs) Well, I never did! Little brown jug's a drop o' rum for your
tea. They're getting right lively on it. *(Coolly)* But you don't come from
round here, do you? . . . *(A distant bell rings, not the front-door bell)* I
come from near Rotherham. Me father works in t'pit, and so does our
Frank and our Wilfred. *(The distant bell sounds again)* . . . *(Coolly)* It's
for me. Let her wait. She's run me off me legs to-day. And Mrs
Northrop's in t'kitchen – she can do a bit for a change. *(She crosses to
Gerald)* There's seven of 'em at it in t'dining-room – Alderman Helliwell
and missus, of course – then Councillor Albert Parker and Mrs Parker,
and Mr Herbert Soppitt and Mrs Soppitt – and of course Miss Holmes
. . . Yes, but she's stopped eating. *(She giggles)* You're courting her, aren't
you? . . . *(Coolly)* Oh – I saw you both – the other night, near Cleckley
Woods. I was out meself, with our milkman's lad . . . Now don't look
like that, I won't tell on you . . . She can't put it away like some of 'em.
I'd rather keep Councillor Albert Parker a week than a fortnight. D'you
want to see her? . . . I'll tell her. *(She turns back)* She'd better come
round that way – through t'greenhouse . . .

Lue – Dartmoor, 20

THE WINTERLING JEZ BUTTERWORTH

First performed at the Royal Court Jerwood Theatre Downstairs, London in 2006.

The action takes place in an abandoned farmhouse in the centre of the forest of Dartmoor in Winter, where 'Draycott' has made a home for himself.

In this scene Draycott has just brought in 'West' – a vagrant who has been sleeping rough for months and is cooking him a meal. When **Lue** comes in carrying a small rucksack and a couple of plastic shopping bags, he asks West to keep her occupied while he goes upstairs to fetch a bottle of scotch.

Lue tells West that she's seen him before at a hostel on the Kerry road, when he told her he was a businessman. She is going abroad and needs someone to sign her passport application.

Published by Nick Hern Books, London

Lue

I need help . . . Filling out forms. A form. I'm going away. I'm going abroad . . . I got everything else. I've got sun cream. And a hat. And sunglasses. And a towel. And a bikini. And a book. I just need to do the form. I just need to fill it out. Get someone to sign it . . . For the passport application . . . *[beat]* Here. *[She takes out a form.]* This isn't the form. This is the form you need to fill out the form. The form form is safe. The form form's upstairs. This is the pre-form. The other one. The orange one. Don't touch it. Your hands are filthy. You smudge it, we're buggered. Here look. *[She reads.]* 'Section One. Form C1. A. One. Please keep these Notes until you receive your passport. Note 1a, subsection one – Birth after 31 December 1982 in the United Kingdom. Tick 'Yes' if you were born after 31 December 1982 in the United Kigndom, or if you entered the country on or before December 31 1989, or after July 1 1992, unless a) you were already a temporary citizen in which case refer to note 2a, subsection seven . . .' And I speak English. That's their opener. That's their warm-up. I mean, that's that. I'm staying put. I ain't going nowhere, am I? Wait for it. *[She searches.]* This is the bit. Where is it? *[Reads.]* 'Note 5a, section three.' No, that's not it. Where is it? Here you go. *[Reads.]* 'Section 12a, subsection 2ii should be signed by a British citizen, or other Commonwealth citizen, who is a Member of Parliament, Justice of the Peace, Minister of Religion, Established Civil Servant, or . . . here we go . . . professionally qualified person in the community, e.g. Businessman, Doctor, blah blah blah, or a person of similar standing.' See? I need someone from the community. Someone they trust. Someone of standing. Now I was thinking, if he was a businessman, or say, or a doctor, then he can do it. Because I figure, he's not been out here long. They probably don't know yet. The government. They probably don't know that he's gibbering in Okehampton Market. What do you reckon? What do you say? . . . I just need you to sign my photo. Sign the form. Read the notes. Say who you are. Vouch for me. I've got everything else. You help me, I won't forget it. You help me, that's that. I'm out of here. You can have my room. You won't freeze to death, out there in your fort. What do you say? Eh? What do you say?

Tina – young

THE WOMAN BEFORE
RICHARD SCHIMMELFENNIG
TRANSLATED BY DAVID TUSHINGHAM

First performed at the Royal Court Theatre, London in 2005.

Frank and his wife Claudia are moving house. As they are packing to leave, a woman arrives on the doorstep and announces that 24 years ago she was Frank's lover and has come to claim him back again. Meanwhile their son, Andi is saying goodbye to his girlfriend, **Tina**.

The action shifts backwards and forwards between scenes, often repeating part of the previous dialogue. It is described as a 'flight of fancy' – but ends with an unexpected and sinister twist

In this scene, **Tina** describes her last evening with Andi, knowing that she will never see him again.

Published by Oberon Modern Plays, London
The full text is currently available from Oberon Books, ISBN: 1840025727.

Tina

We meet as it's getting dark at the top of the bank like we always do, and then we go to the cinema . . . We follow our heroine in submarines, on motorbikes, in jeeps, by parachute, ship, on horseback, suspended from helicopters.

Then we get the bus home . . . I go in the front door, Andi waits down in the garden by my window . . . My room's in the basement. Andi climbs in through the window not making a sound. Everything's quiet.

We lie side by side in my narrow bed in the dark in silence. No music. Above us and around us – like an ancient mausoleum – the house, a small bathroom, my room and the cellar downstairs, the kitchen and the living-room on the ground floor, upstairs my parents' bedroom and a second bathroom.

Just as we are, naked, we start running through the house. Without making a sound we move through the rooms in the dark, along the hall, up and down the stairs. We stand still outside my parents' bedroom and then go on, out of the front door and into the garden, naked despite the cold, onto the lawn and then back downstairs again to my room.

Suddenly my dad's standing in the room in pyjama trousers and a top.

'Out, get out now –' and he grabs hold of Andi and drags him, past my mother who's screaming, up the stairs and throws him out of the house.

I run back down the stairs, lock my door from the inside and climb out of the window with our things. My dad shouts after us.

On the way to his parents' Andi gets the pen out. We put our tag everywhere, on every wall, every drive, every garage door, his name and my name together. Andi and Tina together. The pen passes from him to me and back again. No hearts, just our tag – exactly as we are, side by side, on everything all the way to his.

And then when we're outside the door he says: well then –

Brief pause.

I love you but we'll never see each other again. Yes, I say, I know. Take care. Goodbye.

more ideas *for* speeches: men

Mozart   **AMADEUS** PETER SCHAFFER 130

Carl   **MADAME MELVILLE** RICHARD NELSON 131

Derek   **ONCE A CATHOLIC** MARY O'MALLEY 132

George   **PRESENCE** DAVID HARROWER 133

Andi   **THE WOMAN BEFORE**
ROLAND SCHIMMELPFENNIG 134

Mozart – 20s

AMADEUS PETER SHAFFER

First presented by the National Theatre in London in 1979.

It is set in Vienna in 1823 and in 1781–91, as Salieri, the now elderly Court Composer, recalls his memories of the young genius, **Mozart**, whom he hated so much that he contrived his early demise.

In this scene, **Mozart** is invited to an elite gathering at Salieri's Salon. As the young composer enters, Baron Van Sweiten is criticising **Mozart** for his vulgar choice of subject in 'that disgraceful play, *The Marriage of Figaro*' and is congratulated for his opinion by Von Strack, Groom of the Imperial Chamber.

Published by Penguin Plays

Act II

START: *(Imitating* Von Strack's *drawl)* 'O well said, yes, well said! Exactly! . . .

TO: 'My tongue is stupid. My heart isn't.'

Carl – American, 15

MADAME MELVILLE RICHARD NELSON

First performed at the Vaudeville Theatre, London in October 2000, and set in Paris in 1966. It is the story of **Carl**, a young American boy, and his brief relationship with his literature teacher, the beautiful Claudie Melville.

Claudie invites **Carl** to join her special students who meet twice a week at her apartment to discuss the latest films. One evening she persuades him to stay on after the others have left.

In this scene **Carl** describes their walk along the Quai Du Louvre and Claudie's encounter with his mathematics teacher, Monsieur Darc.

Published by Faber & Faber, London

Page 48
START: 'Outside we walked together along the Quai du Louvre . . .
TO: . . . And then we returned to her apartment.'

Derek – London, late teens

ONCE A CATHOLIC MARY O'MALLEY

First performed at the Royal Court Theatre, London in 1977 and set in the Convent of Our Lady of Fatima – a Grammar School for Girls – and in and around the streets of Willesden and Harlesden, London NW10, from September 1956 to July 1957.

Derek is a Teddy boy with ambitions to become a train driver. He has been going out with fifth-former Mary McGinty for two-and-a-half weeks.

In this scene they are standing on the street corner. He has just tried to kiss her but she turns her head away. 'A passionate kiss on the lips is a serious mortal sin.' Mortal sins mean nothing to **Derek**; he reckons Mary takes her religion a bit too seriously. Mary asks him if he is Church of England.

Published by Amber Lane Press, Oxford

Act I, scene 11

START: 'Yea, that's what I stick down . . .
TO: Spaniards, Portuguese . . .

CUT TO: 'Yea, Bolivians . . .
TO: believe in it, do you?' . . .

CUT TO: 'I know you have to . . .
TO: your own sweet way . . .

CUT TO: 'Yeah, tough . . .
END ON: see you around sometime.'

George – Liverpool, 17
PRESENCE DAVID HARROWER

First presented at the Royal Court Jerwood Theatre in 2001 and set in Hamburg in 1960. A group of three lads from Liverpool – **George**, Pete, and Paul – have been hired to play in the run-down Indra Club for six weeks. Their accommodation consists of a dingy basement room.

In this scene **George** is standing by the wall trying to write a card home to his parents. On the front of the card is a picture of Hamburg. He holds it up to read the inscription to the others.

Published by Faber & Faber, London

Scene 3

START: 'What'm I supposed . . .
TO: eh? . . .

CUT TO: 'The historic port . . .
TO: red hot . . .

CUT TO: 'I wouldn't change . . .
TO: right now . . .

CUT TO: 'Couple of months . . .
TO: exams, eh? . . .

CUT TO: 'Listen, it's . . .
TO: electrician's eyes . . .

CUT TO: 'It's a deathtrap . . .
TO: snap his . . .

CUT TO: 'Like charcoal . . .

CUT TO: 'Just warning you . . .

CUT TO: 'Gives me . . .
TO getting out.'

Andi – young (teens)

THE WOMAN BEFORE
ROLAND SCHIMMELPFENNIG
TRANSLATED BY DAVID TUSHINGHAM

First performance at the Royal Court Jerwood Theatre Downstairs in May 2005.

Frank and his wife are moving home. As they are packing to leave, a woman – Romy – arrives on the doorstep and announces that 24 years ago she was Frank's lover and has come to claim him back. The action shifts backwards and forwards between scenes, often repeating part of the previous dialogue. It is described as 'a flight of fancy' – but ends with a sinister twist.

Frank's son, **Andi**, has just said goodbye to his girlfriend, Tina, knowing he will probably never see her again.

In this scene Romy questions him about his girlfriend. Does he love her? Has he told her so? Will he love her forever? What does she look like?

Published by Oberon Books, London

START: 'Yeah, I said – I'd always love her . . .

CUT TO: 'I'd paint her if I could . . .
TO: high up into the wall . . .

CUT TO: 'Her face . . .

CUT TO: 'Her face is the sky . . .
END: never reach the end, her eyes.'

(brief pause)

more ideas *for* speeches: women

Linda	**ENTER A FREE MAN** TOM STOPPARD	136
Pearl	**HOUSE AND GARDEN** ALAN AYCKBOURN	137
Elke	**PRESENCE** DAVID HARROWER	138
Maire	**TRANSLATIONS** BRIAN FRIEL	139
Pace	**THE TRESTLE AT POPE LICK PARK** NAOMI WALLACE	140

Linda – 18

ENTER A FREE MAN TOM STOPPARD

First performed at the St Martin's Theatre, London in 1968.

When she was young, **Linda** was proud to have an inventor as a father. Now she is fed up with having to provide him with pocket money each week – particularly as he stays upstairs in his room all day 'doing damn all'.

In this scene she is complaining about the situation to her long-suffering mother.

Published by Faber & Faber, London

Act II page 59

START:	'Try to be charitable . . .
TO:	to live in . . .
FROM:	*'Dad!* . . .
TO:	my nerves . . .
FROM:	'I'm not unkind . . .
TO:	what to say . . .
FROM:	'And wash your hands . . .
TO:	a situation, isn't it? . . .
FROM:	'Well, you can't . . .
TO:	half barmy . . .
FROM:	'Shall I call him again? . . .

(omit Persephone's next line)

END:	washed his hands.'

Pearl – 20s

HOUSE AND GARDEN ALAN AYCKBOURN

'GARDEN'

First presented at the Stephen Joseph Theatre, Scarborough in 1999 and at the Royal National Theatre in August 2000.

The action takes place in a large country house and garden. **Pearl** is a member of the domestic staff and is described as a 'casual cleaner'. She is the daughter of the housekeeper; both mother and daughter live with Warn, the gardener.

In this scene **Pearl** brings Warn his elevenses. Throughout her dialogue he shows little interest and is either feeling the grass or looking up at the sky.

Published by Faber & Faber, London

Act I, scene 1

START: 'Here. Brought you your 'levenses . . .
TO: normal people . . .

FROM: 'Bloody garden fêtes . . .
END: clean it out.'

Elke – German but with American accent; young

PRESENCE DAVID HARROWER

First presented at the Royal Court Jerwood Theatre Upstairs in 2001 and set in Hamburg in 1960.

A pop group from Liverpool have been booked to play in Hamburg at the run-down Indra Club. On their night off they are drinking in the bar 'Gemini', and make friends with a young barmaid, **Elke**, who joins them at their table. She tells them she is not happy working in Hamburg, and one of the group asks her why she doesn't go back to America.

Published by Faber & Faber, London

Scene 8

START: 'I'm German . . .
(omitting George and Paul's line throughout the speech)
TO: He's a Nazi . . .

FROM: 'He wasn't SS or anything . . .
END: Something to get rid of the taste.'

Note: This is a useful example of a speech broken up by one line comments from other characters.

Maire – Irish – Donegal; young

TRANSLATIONS BRIAN FRIEL

First presented by the Field Day Theatre Company in the Guildhall, Derry in 1980.

The action takes place in 1833 in a hedge-school in Baile Beg, an Irish-speaking community in County Donegal. A detachment of the Royal Engineers have arrived to make the first ordnance survey, and Lieutenant George Yolland has the task of changing the place-names. He meets and falls in love with **Maire** – a young girl who attends the hedge-school and works on a nearby farm.

In this scene **Maire** arrives at the school carrying a pail of milk. She hasn't seen Yolland since the previous night and he failed to report for work that morning. She is distraught. He would never have gone away without letting her know.

Published by Faber & Faber, London

Act III

START:	'Honest to God . . .
TO:	and isn't it empty . . .
FROM:	'(Yolland) left me home, Owen . . .
TO:	What do you think? . . .
FROM:	'He comes from a tiny wee place . . .
END:	it didn't last long, did it?'

Pace – American, 17

THE TRESTLE AT POPE LICK PARK
NAOMI WALLACE

First performed at the Humana Festival, Louisville in 1998 and at the Traverse Theatre, Edinburgh in 2001.

Sixteen-year-old Dalton Chase is alone in a prison cell, haunted by the image of **Pace Creagen** whom he is accused of killing. In flash-back he sees her running to meet him under the trestle at Pope Lick Creek. She has run it before on her own. Her second attempt with her friend, Brett, ended in disaster.

In this scene **Pace** describes the moment leading up to Brett being struck by the train. Dalton says it was stupid.

Published by Faber & Faber, London

Act I, scene 10

START:	'Yeah, it was . . .
TO:	Brett was right behind me . . .
FROM:	'I thought he was running . . .
TO:	'Cause it will . . .
FROM:	'Just stood there . . .
TO:	going to flinch . . .
FROM:	'It's not how you think . . .
TO:	cut Brett in two . . .
FROM:	'You know . . .
END:	Whole.'

useful addresses

The Actors' Theatre School
32 Exeter Road
London NW2 4SB
Tel: 020 8450 0371
Fax: 020 8450 1057

Offstage Bookshop
at Treadwells
34 Tavistock Street
London WC2E 7PB
Tel: 020 7240 3883

Tona de Brett
020 7372 6179

Sylvia Carson
020 8422 5026

Laine Theatre Arts
The Studios
East Street
Epsom KT17 1HH
Tel: 01372 724648
Fax: 01372 723775

Polka Theatre For Children
240 The Broadway
Wimbledon
London SW19 1SB

The British Library
96 Euston Road
London NW1 2DB
Tel: 020 7412 7676

The Academy Drama School
189 Whitechapel Road
London E1 1DN
Tel: 020 7377 8735

The American Academy
of Dramatic Arts
120 Madison Avenue
New York NY 10016
Tel: 212 686 9244
Fax: 212 679 8752

The Royal Academy of
Dramatic Art
62/64 Gower Street
London WC1E 6ED
Tel: 020 7373 9883

London Academy of Music and
Dramatic Art (LAMDA)
Tower House
226 Cromwell Road
London SW5 0SR
Tel: 020 7373 9883

Streets Alive
www.streetsalive.org.uk

The City Literary Institute
Stukeley Street
Drury Lane
London WC2B 5LJ
Tel: 020 7430 0544

copyright holders

Agnes of God by John Pielmeier
Copyright © 1982 by Courage Productions Inc.

Ah! Wilderness by Eugene O'Neill
Published by Jonathan Cape. Reprinted by permission of The Random House Group Ltd.

Another Country by Julian Mitchell
Copyright © Julian Mitchell 1982. Reproduced by permission of Amber Lane Press.

Back to Methuselah by George Bernard Shaw
Reproduced by permission of The Society of Authors, on behalf of the Bernard Shaw Estate.

A Brief History of Helen of Troy by Marz Schultz
Reproduced by permission of Oberon Books.

The Corn is Green by Emlyn Williams
Copyright © Emlyn Williams 1941.

Cressida by Nicholas Wright
An excerpt (abridged) from *Cressida* by Nicholas Wright. Published by Nick Hern Books, The Glasshouse, 49a Goldhawk Road, London W12 8QP.

Fanny's First Play by George Bernard Shaw
Reproduced by permission of The Society of Authors, on behalf of the Bernard Shaw Estate.

Flatmates by Ellen Dryden
Published by First Writes Books and reproduced by permission. Subject to copyright. Please contact directly for professional and amateur performance rights.

The Glass Menagerie by Tennessee Williams
Copyright © 1945 by the University of the South and Edwin D. Williams. Reprinted by permission of New Directions Publishing Corp.